SUSTAINABLE AMERICA

A NEW CONSENSUS FOR PROSPERITY, OPPORTUNITY, AND A HEALTHY ENVIRONMENT FOR THE FUTURE

FEBRUARY 1996

THE PRESIDENT'S COUNCIL ON SUSTAINABLE DEVELOPMENT

5/96

The President's Council on Sustainable Development is actively seeking suggestions for improving federal policies related to advancing sustainable development. We encourage you to send your ideas to this address:

President's Council on Sustainable Development
730 Jackson Place, NW
Washington, DC 20503
Our e-mail address is: pcsd@igc.apc.org

For sale by the U.S. Government Printing Office
Superintendent of Documents, Mail Stop: SSOP, Washington, DC 20402-9328
ISBN 0-16-048529-0

Neither the Council nor the President alone can bring about change in the United States. Change will not and cannot come alone from Washington to the country, although Washington must provide leadership. The work of the Council will be important only if it ignites many debates; helps to inspire independent action; and encourages business, citizens, and government to invent new forms of dialogue and interaction.

The President's idea of appointing "industry" and "environmental" co-chairs for a Council that included members of his cabinet as well as leaders from many sectors of society presented us with an unusual challenge. We hardly knew each other when we started. The "environmentalist" had experience as a regulatory official, environmental litigator, and sharp critic of the company in which the "industrialist" has spent his professional life. Now we had to agree — and learn to trust each other — to be able to lead the Council.

Over the past three years we have given dozens of speeches together, held joint press conferences, met with hundreds of citizens — some of whom had harsh words and deep suspicion of one or the other of us because of our background. We have chaired scores of meetings and spent countless hours debating how to help the Council succeed. Through all this, we have developed a warm friendship and a capacity to find a genuine and productive congruence of views on most any issue. We have sometimes lost track of which of us was the executive and which the environmentalist, and, indeed, after one speech to a Rotary Club even our audience was confused.

The meetings of the Council have been public, and we have invited hundreds of people from dozens of communities to address us. Often, community leaders and local activists moved the Council ahead by voicing a cogent mix of vision and pragmatism, concern for the future, and conviction that people can find sensible solutions. We thank them. They helped us greatly. We hope our report helps them.

Finally, we want to offer our thanks and earnest appreciation to the Council's executive director, Molly Harriss Olson, and her bright, dedicated staff, and to express our great gratitude and admiration for the members of the Council. We have watched with deepening respect as the members set aside their preconceptions and approached hard issues with openness and honesty. We have been touched by their eloquence and conviction. We have enjoyed their humor and valued their forbearance. They confronted the question, "What are our hopes and how do we meet our responsibility to the future?" with courage, intelligence, and integrity. We thank them for having made it such a privilege to work with them.

Jonathan Lash
President
World Resources Institute

David T. Buzzelli
Vice President
The Dow Chemical Company

8 We need a new collaborative decision process that leads to better decisions; more rapid change; and more sensible use of human, natural, and financial resources in achieving our goals.

9 The nation must strengthen its communities and enhance their role in decisions about environment, equity, natural resources, and economic progress so that the individuals and institutions most immediately affected can join with others in the decision process.

10 Economic growth, environmental protection, and social equity are linked. We need to develop integrated policies to achieve these national goals.

11 The United States should have policies and programs that contribute to stabilizing global human population; this objective is critical if we hope to have the resources needed to ensure a high quality of life for future generations.

12 Even in the face of scientific uncertainty, society should take reasonable actions to avert risks where the potential harm to human health or the environment is thought to be serious or irreparable.

13 Steady advances in science and technology are essential to help improve economic efficiency, protect and restore natural systems, and modify consumption patterns.

14 A growing economy and healthy environment are essential to national and global security.

15 A knowledgeable public, the free flow of information, and opportunities for review and redress are critically important to open, equitable, and effective decisionmaking.

16 Citizens must have access to high-quality and lifelong formal and nonformal education that enables them to understand the interdependence of economic prosperity, environmental quality, and social equity — and prepares them to take actions that support all three.

INTRODUCTION

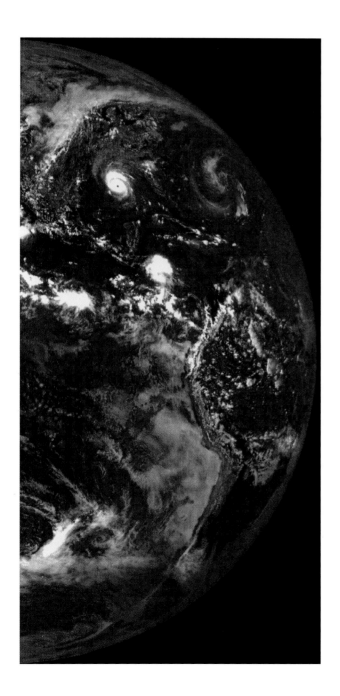

President Clinton asked the Council to recommend a national action strategy for sustainable development at a time when Americans are confronted with new challenges that have global ramifications. The Council concluded that in order to meet the needs of the present while ensuring that future generations have the same opportunities, the United States must change by moving from conflict to collaboration and adopting stewardship and individual responsibility as tenets by which to live.

IN JUNE 1993, when President Clinton created the President's Council on Sustainable Development, he asked us to find ways "to bring people together to meet the needs of the present without jeopardizing the future."[1] He gave us a task that required us to think about the future and about the consequences of the choices this generation makes on the lives of future generations. It is a task that has caused each of us to think about human needs, economic prosperity, and human interactions with nature differently than we had before.

The recommendations in this report are not only for government, but also for the private sector and citizens since government by itself cannot overcome apathy, spur innovation, or inspire new values.

No one can predict the future — how people will live, or what exactly they will need — but it is possible to foresee the likely effects of some of today's decisions and to make choices that honor the interests of present and future generations. In the nearly three years of the Council's work, in our meetings across the country, we heard concern that despite America's great wealth, power, and technological prowess, Americans cannot assume that the future of their children's lives will be better than the present. Those who met with us see, as we do, trends that lead in troubling directions and opportunities that must soon be seized or lost.

We view this challenge with considerable optimism because the potential benefits of knowledge are essentially inexhaustible; because global attention to developing sustainably is growing; and because many communities, companies, and individuals are independently taking first steps toward responding to the need for change.

But optimism is not complacency. Opportunities for change and anecdotes of progress do not by themselves redirect global trends. There are substantial obstacles to overcome that require conscious and concerted action, sometimes by government, sometimes by the private sector, or sometimes by citizens in communities or as individuals — but often, all sectors need to be actively involved. The recommendations in this report are not only for government, but also for the private sector and citizens since government by itself cannot overcome apathy, spur innovation, or inspire new values.

NEW CHALLENGES FOR AMERICANS

These are remarkable times. This is an era of rapid and often bewildering alterations in the forces and conditions that shape human life. This is evident both in the altered nature of geopolitics in the post-Cold War era and in the growing understanding of the relationship between human beings and the natural world.

The end of the Cold War has been accompanied by the swift advance of democracy in places where it was previously unknown and an even more rapid spread of market-based economies. The authority of central governments is eroding, and power has begun to shift to local governments and private institutions. In some countries, freedom and opportunity are flourishing, while in others these changes have unleashed the violence of old conflicts and new ambitions.

Internationally, trade, investment, information, and even people flow across borders largely outside of governmental control. Domestically, deregulation and the shift of responsibilities from federal to state and local governments are changing the relationships among levels of government and between government and the private sector.

Communications technology has enhanced people's ability to receive information and influence events that affect them. This has sparked explosive growth in the number of organizations, associations, and networks formed by citizens, businesses, and communities seeking a greater voice for their interests. As a result, society outside of government — civil society — is demanding a greater role in governmental decisions, while at the same time impatiently seeking solutions outside government's power to decide.

But technological innovation is changing much more than communication. It is changing the ways in which Americans live, work, produce, and consume. Knowledge has become the economy's most important and dynamic resource. It has rapidly improved efficiency as those who create and sell goods and services substitute information and innovation for raw materials. During the past 20 years, the amount of energy and natural resources the U.S. economy uses to produce each constant dollar of output has steadily declined, as have many forms of pollution.[2] When U.S. laws first required industry to control pollution, the response was to install cleanup equipment. The shift to a knowledge-driven economy has emphasized the positive connection among efficiency, profits, and environmental protection and helped launch a trend in profitable pollution prevention. More Americans now know that pollution is waste, waste is inefficient, and inefficiency is expensive.

Even as their access to information and to means of communication have increased, citizens of wealthy industrialized nations are becoming cynical about, and frustrated with, traditional political arrangements that no longer seem responsive to their needs. The confidence of many Americans in the large institutions that affect their lives — such as business; government; the media; and environmental, labor, and civic organizations — is eroding. Individual citizens have lost faith in their ability to influence events and have surrendered to apathy, or, worse, to anger. We saw striking contrasts between communities struggling with disaffection and despair, and communities where energized and optimistic citizens have become engaged in shaping their own future.

Bringing about positive change is the challenge that the United States, and we as a Council, face. We believe that significant change is both necessary and inevitable. American society has been characterized by its capacity to embrace and profit from change. But how can communities be mobilized to leave future generations a cleaner, more resilient environment; a more prosperous nation; a more equitable society; and a more productive and efficient economy — one that is competitive internationally? The situation is especially difficult because the pace and extent of today's changes are unprecedented, reflecting the local consequences of the interaction of economic, social, and environmental forces at the global level.

GLOBAL CHANGES THAT AFFECT US ALL

Since the end of World War II, the world's economic output has increased substantially, allowing widespread improvements in health, education, and opportunity, but also creating growing disparities between rich and poor. Even within wealthy nations, including the United States, the gap between rich and poor is widening.[3]

Prosperity, fairness, and a healthy environment are interrelated elements of the human dream of a better future. Sustainable development is a way to pursue that dream through choice and policy.

Tomorrow's world will be shaped by the aspirations of a much larger global population. The number of people living on Earth has doubled in the last 50 years; the equivalent of the population of the United States was added to the world total during the course of this Council's work.[4]

Growing populations demand more food, goods, services, and space. Where there is scarcity, population increase aggravates it. Where there is conflict, rising demand for land and natural resources exacerbates it. Struggling to survive in places that can no longer sustain them, growing populations overfish, overharvest, and overgraze.

Economic growth and innovations in agricultural technology allow many of the world's people to improve their lives as global population increases, but growth and improvement are not without consequences to the Earth's natural systems. Some of the resources used, such as minerals and fossil fuels, while plentiful, are finite; once used, they are exhausted and cannot be renewed. Living resources — plants, animals, and fish — are renewable, but can be destroyed. Human ingenuity has developed alternatives for scarce resources, but that does not mean that depletion of resources has been — or will be — free of serious human and natural consequences. In fact, the demands of a growing human population and an expanding global economy are placing increasing stresses on natural systems.

And while the exhaustion of finite resources may result in human and economic dislocation, the destruction of renewable resources often has far broader ramifications because they are part of a dynamic and interdependent natural system. When a forest is destroyed, species lose their habitat and disappear. The resulting erosion affects river and coastal resources, and, in many cases, rainfall patterns change.

In the late 20th century, the effects of human activity on natural systems are not only visible, they are observable from year to year. In the 130 years from 1850 to 1980, about 15 percent of the world's forests disappeared. During the next 10 years, another 6 percent — an area larger than California, Texas, New York, and Montana combined — was cut and not replanted.[5] The expansion of human population and the destruction of forests, grasslands, wetlands, and river systems bring an accelerated loss of species diversity. This diversity is the source not only of a wide range of human benefits — 25 percent of new medicines, for example — but also the key to the ecosystem's resilience in the face of change.[6] The pressures on natural resources are myriad. For example, pollution, coastal development, and intense fishing reduce ocean fish stocks. While the number and size of fishing fleets are increasing worldwide, fish harvests are falling.[7] Human activity, primarily the burning of coal, oil, and gas, releases pollutants that are changing the chemistry of the Earth's atmosphere — changes that may eventually affect the Earth's climate.

Economic growth has often been accompanied by pollution, affecting both human health and the environment. Even though many wealthy nations have made remarkable progress in reducing pollution, the focus of industrial expansion has shifted to developing nations where environmental protection sometimes may not be regarded as affordable. Even though pollution controls and efficiency in developed nations have started to offset some of the global effects of growth, global pollution is increasing.

Because global economic, social, and environmental trends are connected, Americans' hopes for the future are linked to the rest of the world. Americans compete in a global economy shaped by global trends. American power and interests are global in nature, and the lives of Americans are affected by global environmental changes. The United States, with its high standard of living, is the largest producer and consumer of goods and services, and the largest producer of wastes on Earth.[8] What Americans do affects the lives of people in every nation, and changes in their lives eventually affect Americans.

The U.S. economy, although still the world's largest, is no longer dominant; it is part of a global marketplace. U.S. enterprises can no longer thrive by looking only to domestic markets and domestic competitors. The fastest growing markets are not in the industrialized countries, but in those countries whose economies are in the process of becoming industrialized. Banks and private investors create huge international capital flows, seeking opportunities wherever they occur. Exports represent 7.3 percent of the U.S. gross domestic product. Imports are 9.5 percent of U.S. consumption. Burgeoning international trade now exceeds $4 trillion per year. International currency trading exceeds $1 trillion per day.[9]

The paradoxical challenge that the United States and the world face at the end of the 20th century is to generate individual economic opportunities and national wealth necessary for economically healthy societies while, at the same time, lessening the environmental risks and social inequities that have accompanied past economic development. Both in the world and in the United States, there will be more people and they will aspire to better lives. Responding to those aspirations, particularly if prevalent patterns of consumption continue, will require the production of more goods and services. The challenge of sustainable development is to find ways to meet those needs without destroying the resources upon which future progress depends.

PURSUIT OF COMMON GOALS

Prosperity, fairness, and a healthy environment are interralated elements of the human dream of a better future. Sustainable development is a way to pursue that dream through choice and policy. Work, wealth, community, and the environment are interwoven into the fabric of everyday life and the life of the nation. Sustainable development is the framework that integrates economic, environmental, and social goals in discourse and policies that enhance the prospects of human aspirations.

The Council had hard and frequent debates about the term economic growth, and heard it discussed by members of the public as well, at almost all of our meetings. In the end, we found agreement around the idea that to achieve our vision of sustainability some things must grow — jobs, productivity, wages, profits, capital and savings, information, knowledge, education — and others — pollution, waste, poverty, energy and material use per unit of output — must not. We agree on growth, and agree that it must be defined and measured with care. The issue is not whether the economy needs to grow but how and in what way.

An economy that creates good jobs and safeguards public health and the environment will be stronger and more resilient than one that does not. A country that protects its ecosystems and manages its natural resources wisely lays a far stronger base for future prosperity than one that carelessly uses its assets and destroys its natural capital. A society that invests in its children and communities, equitably providing education and opportunity, is far more likely to prosper than one that does not make such investments and allows the gap between rich and poor to widen.

By recognizing that economic, environmental, and social goals are integrally linked and by having policies that reflect that interrelationship, Americans can regain their sense that they are in control of their future and that the lives of each generation will be better than the last. Thinking narrowly about jobs, energy, transportation, housing, or ecosystems — as if they were not connected — creates new problems even as it attempts to solve old ones. Asking the wrong questions is a sure way to get misleading answers that result in short-term remedies for symptoms, instead of cures for long-term basic problems.

Seeing choices in terms of tradeoffs and balance reflects a history of confrontational politics. It pits vital necessities against each other in a false contest that inhibits exploration of the best solutions, those that link economic gain, ecological improvement, social equity, and well-being — solutions that build common purpose from shared goals.

The United States is a democracy with powerful traditions of individual liberty. What happens in American society ultimately depends on the values that guide the choices that individuals make — which is a function of their commitment and understanding. People act according to their perception of the intersection of their needs and wants, their values and conditions, and the events that affect them. But the narrow and immediate interests of individuals, organizations, or government officials do not necessarily coincide with the long-term interests of a larger community at home or abroad. Although people can act in the interests of the larger community, they rarely do so alone. Because each fears losing separately, all lose together.

MOVING FORWARD:
FROM CONFLICT TO COLLABORATION

How can more than 261 million individual Americans define and reconcile their needs and aspirations with community values and the needs of the future? Our most important finding is the potential power of and growing desire for decision processes that promote direct and meaningful interaction involving people in decisions that affect them. Americans want to take back control of their lives. Communities throughout the country are demonstrating that it is possible to shift from conflict to collaboration when citizens find common values to guide community action. Trust can be restored, hope can be expanded, and people can find ways to lead prosperous lives in harmony with the environment.

Throughout this report, there are recommendations to create structures that will involve more people and a broader range of interests in shaping community vision and making public policy. These will improve decisions, mitigate conflict, and begin to counteract the corrosive trends of cynicism and civic disengagement that afflict society.

More collaborative approaches to making decisions can be arduous and time-consuming (as we have learned over the past nearly three years), and all of the players must change their customary roles. For government, this means using its power to convene and facilitate, shifting gradually from prescribing behavior to supporting responsibility by setting goals, creating incentives, monitoring performance, and providing information.

> *Our most important finding is the potential power of and growing desire for decision processes that promote direct and meaningful interaction involving people in decisions that affect them.*

The federal government, in particular, can help set boundaries for and facilitate place-based policy dialogues. These are dialogues that focus on the resources and management of conflicts of particular places or regions while giving more opportunity, power, and responsibility to communities to address natural resource questions that affect them directly and primarily.

For their part, businesses need to build the practice and skills of dialogue with communities and citizens, participating in community decisionmaking and opening their own values, strategies, and performance to their community and the society.

Advocates, too, must accept the burdens and constraints of rational dialogue built on trust, and communities must create open and inclusive debates about their future.

STEWARDSHIP AS A GUIDE

Stewardship is an invaluable guide to action. Members of the Council were powerfully moved by testimony from a group of senior clergy and lay leaders representing a remarkably broad spectrum of religious groups. They said that the call to care for the Earth is an inescapable component and a rigorous standard of faith. It is a human impulse as well as a moral imperative. In so many modes — intuitive, aesthetic, spiritual, religious — humans know that by protecting the Earth, they find a sense of place and purpose and fulfill a moral obligation to the future.

The intuitive and essentially moral commitment Americans have to preserving Earth's beauty and productivity for future generations is best expressed in the concept of stewardship. Principles of stewardship help define appropriate human interaction with the natural world. Stewardship is more a perspective than a science; it is a set of values that applies to a variety of decisions. It provides moral standards that cannot be imposed but can be taught, encouraged, and reinforced. Instilled in individuals and institutions, it can motivate resolve for voluntary change. Principles of stewardship can illuminate complex policy choices and guide individuals toward the common good.

Stewardship is a workable perspective for all professions. For government, it can refocus policy on the long-term needs of the economy. For advocates, it can mean embracing the needs for prosperity, environmental protection, and social equity and well-being. For corporate America, it can profitably shape a business' strategic vision and inform decisions on the shop floor. For families, it can provide a framework for rethinking customs of consumption. This report suggests a variety of means to inform, encourage, reward, and support stewardship.

INDIVIDUAL RESPONSIBILITY

Another important emphasis of the report is on individual responsibility. No set of policies, no system of incentives, no amount of information can substitute for individual responsibility or counteract apathy. Information can provide a basis for action. Vision and ideas can influence perceptions and inspire change. New ways to make decisions can empower those who seek a role in shaping the future. However, our recommendations will be meaningless unless individuals acting as citizens, consumers, investors, managers, workers, and professionals decide that it is important to them to make choices on the basis of a broader, longer view of their self-interest; to get involved in turning those choices into action; and, most importantly, to be held accountable for their actions.

The combination of political will, technological innovation, and a very large investment of resources and human ingenuity in pursuit of environmental goals has produced enormous benefits for Americans. This is an achievement to celebrate, but in a world and a nation that steadily uses more materials to make more goods for more people, we recognize that we will have to achieve more in the future for the sake of the future. We foresee a world in which zero waste will become an ideal for society even as zero defects has become so for manufacturing.

We are convinced that the change in the form and nature of the civic discussion that we propose can make the issues of sustainability a bridge between people and institutions. That, we believe, is the essence of sustainable development: the recognition that the pursuit of one set of goals affects others and that we must pursue policies that integrate economic, environmental, and social goals.

CHAPTER 1

NATIONAL GOALS TOWARD SUSTAINABLE DEVELOPMENT

This common set of goals emerged from the Council's vision. These goals express in concrete terms the elements of sustainability. Alongside the goals are suggested indicators that can be used to help measure progress toward achieving them.

THE FOLLOWING GOALS express the shared aspirations of the President's Council on Sustainable Development. They are truly interdependent and flow from the Council's understanding that it is essential to seek economic prosperity, environmental protection, and social equity together. The achievement of any one goal is not enough to ensure that future generations will have at least the same opportunities to live and prosper that this generation enjoys: all are needed.

GOAL 1: HEALTH AND THE ENVIRONMENT

Ensure that every person enjoys the benefits of clean air, clean water, and a healthy environment at home, at work, and at play.

GOAL 2: ECONOMIC PROSPERITY

Sustain a healthy U.S. economy that grows sufficiently to create meaningful jobs, reduce poverty, and provide the opportunity for a high quality of life for all in an increasingly competitive world.

GOAL 3: EQUITY

Ensure that all Americans are afforded justice and have the opportunity to achieve economic, environmental, and social well-being.

GOAL 4: CONSERVATION OF NATURE

Use, conserve, protect, and restore natural resources — land, air, water, and biodiversity — in ways that help ensure long-term social, economic, and environmental benefits for ourselves and future generations.

GOAL 5: STEWARDSHIP

Create a widely held ethic of stewardship that strongly encourages individuals, institutions, and corporations to take full responsibility for the economic, environmental, and social consequences of their actions.

GOAL 6: SUSTAINABLE COMMUNITIES

Encourage people to work together to create healthy communities where natural and historic resources are preserved, jobs are available, sprawl is contained, neighborhoods are secure, education is lifelong, transportation and health care are accessible, and all citizens have opportunities to improve the quality of their lives.

GOAL 7: CIVIC ENGAGEMENT

Create full opportunity for citizens, businesses, and communities to participate in and influence the natural resource, environmental, and economic decisions that affect them.

GOAL 8: POPULATION

Move toward stabilization of U.S. population.

GOAL 9: INTERNATIONAL RESPONSIBILITY

>Take a leadership role in the development and implementation of global sustainable development policies, standards of conduct, and trade and foreign policies that further the achievement of sustainability.

GOAL 10: EDUCATION

>Ensure that all Americans have equal access to education and lifelong learning opportunities that will prepare them for meaningful work, a high quality of life, and an understanding of the concepts involved in sustainable development.

Accompanying the goals are indicators of progress, yardsticks to measure progress toward each goal. These indicators of progress suggest what information to look at to determine the progress that the country is making toward achieving the goals. They are not intended to be mandates for specific actions or policies, and they may change over time as the country moves toward these goals and learns more about the science and policy options underlying them. Graphics illustrating a few possible indicators are included. In some cases, the suggested indicators are concepts that are not now easily measured and will require more work before they can be used as true yardsticks.

GOAL 1

HEALTH AND THE ENVIRONMENT

Ensure that every person enjoys the benefits of clean air, clean water, and a healthy environment at home, at work, and at play.

FIGURE 1

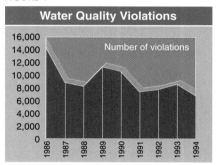

SOURCE: The National Public Water System Supervision Program, *FY 1994 National Compliance Report.*

INDICATORS OF PROGRESS

Clean air, clean water, and reduced exposure to toxics are basic indicators. Beyond that, other environmental exposures (such as to lead and tobacco smoke) can also contribute directly and indirectly to health problems. Where causal links can be identified, additional indicators should be used.

CLEAN AIR

Decreased number of people living in areas that fail to meet air quality standards.

DRINKING WATER

Decreased number of people whose drinking water fails to meet national safe drinking water standards.

TOXIC EXPOSURES

Reduced releases that contribute to human exposure to toxic materials.

DISEASES AND MORTALITY

Decrease in diseases and deaths from environmental exposures, including occupationally related illnesses.

GOAL 2

INDICATORS OF PROGRESS

ECONOMIC PROSPERITY

Sustain a healthy U.S. economy that grows sufficiently to create meaningful jobs, reduce poverty, and provide the opportunity for a high quality of life for all in an increasingly competitive world.

The traditional measures of economic activity include gross domestic product (GDP), net domestic product (NDP), and the unemployment rate. These measures, however, do not take into account negative environmental impacts of production and consumption or gauge the incidence of poverty. The Council agreed that additional yardsticks are needed for adequately gauging economic progress in the broadest sense.

ECONOMIC PERFORMANCE
Increases in per capita GDP and NDP.

EMPLOYMENT
Increases in the number, wage level, and quality of jobs (as measured, for example, by the percentage of jobs at or below minimum wage).

POVERTY
Decreased number of people living below the poverty line.

SAVINGS AND INVESTMENT RATES
Higher per capita savings and investment rates.

NATURAL RESOURCES AND ENVIRONMENTAL ACCOUNTING
Development and use of new economic measures or satellite accounts that reflect resource depletion and environmental costs.

PRODUCTIVITY
Increased per capita production per hour worked.

FIGURE 2

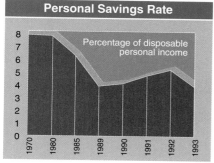

SOURCE: U.S. Department of Commerce, *Statistical Abstract of the United States 1994* (Washington, D.C.: Government Printing Office, 1994).

GOAL 3   INDICATORS OF PROGRESS

EQUITY

Ensure that all Americans are afforded justice and have the opportunity to achieve economic, environmental, and social well-being.

FIGURE 3

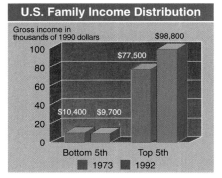

SOURCE: World Resources Institute, Resources and Environmental Information Program, Washington, D.C., 1995.

The Council believes that equity is such an important goal that it has worked to weave this priority into each element of this report. However, measuring fairness and equality of opportunity throughout a population is complex. It requires measuring differences between rich and poor in a number of ways and involves yardsticks not yet available. Such measures should be developed to show whether the nation is progressing toward greater equity by reducing disparities in risks and access to benefits.

INCOME TRENDS

Increase in the average income of the bottom 20 percent compared with that of the top 20 percent of the U.S. population.

ENVIRONMENTAL EQUITY

Development of measures of any disproportionate environmental burdens (such as exposure to air, water, and toxic pollution) borne by different economic and social groups.

SOCIAL EQUITY

Development of measures of access to critical services (such as education, health care, and community services), and opportunities to participate in decisionmaking by different economic and social groups, such as the percentage of these populations attending college.

GOAL 4

INDICATORS OF PROGRESS

CONSERVATION OF NATURE

Use, conserve, protect, and restore natural resources — land, air, water, and biodiversity — in ways that help ensure long-term social, economic, and environmental benefits for ourselves and future generations.

Measuring the health and extent of natural systems is difficult because they are complex; vary over time and space; and have effects that can be local, regional, and/or global. Most of the following indicators focus on local and regional systems, reflecting the Council's work on watersheds and communities. Additional indicators are needed to reflect how well the nation is contributing to the protection of natural systems worldwide.

ECOSYSTEMS

Increase in the health of ecosystems, including forests, grasslands, wetlands, surface waters, and coastal lands:

- Decreased soil loss and associated productivity loss due to erosion and chemical or biological changes in natural systems and other lands such as agricultural lands.
- Increased number of acres of healthy wetlands.
- Increased percentage of forests managed to reach full maturity and diversity.
- Development of indicators to measure water bodies with healthy biological communities.
- Increased number of acres of healthy native grasslands.

FIGURE 4

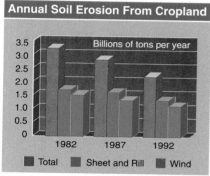

SOURCE: U.S. Department of Agriculture, Natural Resources Conservation Service, *Summary Report, 1992 — National Resources Inventory* (Washington, D.C., 1995).

HABITAT LOSS

Development of measures of threats to habitat loss and the extent of habitat conversion, such as the rate of wetlands loss.

THREATENED AND ENDANGERED SPECIES

Decreased number of threatened and endangered species.

NUTRIENTS AND TOXICS

Decreased releases that contribute to the exposure of natural systems to toxics and excess nutrients.

EXOTIC SPECIES

Reduced ecological impacts caused by the introduction and spread of exotic species.

GLOBAL ENVIRONMENTAL CHANGE

Reduced emissions of greenhouse gases and of compounds that damage the ozone layer.

GOAL 5

STEWARDSHIP

Create a widely held ethic of stewardship that strongly encourages individuals, institutions, and corporations to take full responsibility for the economic, environmental, and social consequences of their actions.

FIGURE 5

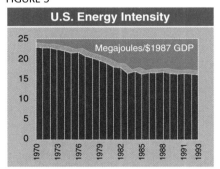

U.S. Energy Intensity
Megajoules/$1987 GDP

SOURCE: World Resources Institute, Resources and Environmental Information Program, Washington, D.C., 1995.

INDICATORS OF PROGRESS

Stewardship is an ethic or value; quantitative measures of it are difficult and need further work. What can be readily measured is the use of natural resources within the United States — efficient use and wise management are key to ensuring that such resources will be available for future generations.

MATERIALS CONSUMPTION
Increased efficiency of materials use, such as materials intensity measured per capita or per unit of output.

WASTE REDUCTION
Increased source reduction, reuse, recovery, and recycling.

ENERGY EFFICIENCY
Reduced energy intensity (energy per unit output).

RENEWABLE RESOURCE USE
Decreased rate of harvest or use compared to rate of regeneration in fisheries, forests, soil, and groundwater.

GOAL 6

SUSTAINABLE COMMUNITIES

Encourage people to work together to create healthy communities where natural and historic resources are preserved, jobs are available, sprawl is contained, neighborhoods are secure, education is lifelong, transportation and health care are accessible, and all citizens have opportunities to improve the quality of their lives.

FIGURE 6

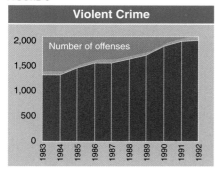

SOURCE: *Statistical Abstract of the United States 1994.*

INDICATORS OF PROGRESS

Local values and priorities shape the characteristics that contribute to strong and stable communities. However, thriving communities across the nation share many common traits as do threatened communities. Indicators need to allow for diversity among communities while recognizing national priorities.

COMMUNITY ECONOMIC VIABILITY

Increased local per capita income and employment in urban, suburban, and rural communities.

SAFE NEIGHBORHOODS

Decrease in violent crime rates.

PUBLIC PARKS

Increase in urban green space, park space, and recreational areas.

INVESTMENT IN FUTURE GENERATIONS

Increase in the amount of public and private resources dedicated to children, including health care, maternal care, childhood development, and education and training.

TRANSPORTATION PATTERNS

Decrease in measures of traffic congestion; increase in the use of public and alternative transportation systems.

COMMUNITY ACCESS TO INFORMATION

Increase in library use and the percentage of schools and libraries with access to the Internet and National Information Infrastructure.

SHELTER

Decreased number of homeless people by community.

METROPOLITAN INCOME PATTERNS

Reduced disparity in per capita income between urban areas and their suburbs.

INFANT MORTALITY

Decrease in infant mortality rates by economic and social group.

GOAL 7

INDICATORS OF PROGRESS

CIVIC ENGAGEMENT

Create full opportunity for citizens, businesses, and communities to participate in and influence the natural resource, environmental, and economic decisions that affect them.

Democratic societies rely on an engaged population of diverse individuals and institutions. Additional measures are needed to track participation and gauge the effectiveness of policies that strengthen cooperative decisionmaking while still allowing for individual leadership and creativity. Effective yardsticks may come from studying successful efforts to build community values, public trust, and government responsiveness.

PUBLIC PARTICIPATION
Increase in the percentage of eligible voters who cast ballots in national, state, and local elections.

New indicators must be developed to measure:

SOCIAL CAPITAL
Increase in citizen engagement and public trust, such as the willingness of people in a community to cooperate for their mutual benefit.

CITIZEN PARTICIPATION
Increase in community participation in such civic activities as professional and service organizations, parent-teacher associations, sporting leagues, and volunteer work.

COLLABORATIONS
Increased use of successful civic collaborations such as public-private partnerships, community-based planning and goal-setting projects, and consensus-building efforts.

FIGURE 7

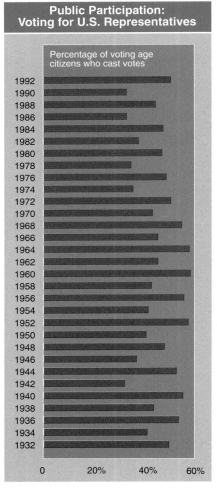

Public Participation:
Voting for U.S. Representatives

Percentage of voting age citizens who cast votes

SOURCE: *Statistical Abstract of the United States 1994.*

GOAL 8

POPULATION

Move toward stabilization of U.S. population.

FIGURE 8

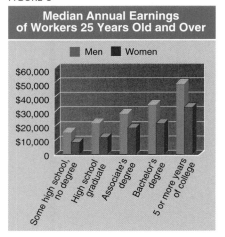

Median Annual Earnings of Workers 25 Years Old and Over

Men Women

SOURCE: U.S. Department of Commerce, *Statistical Abstract of the United States 1993* (Washington, D.C.: Government Printing Office, 1994).

INDICATORS OF PROGRESS

Together with the more traditional population measurements, such as estimates of growth, trends and measures of the social and economic status of women within society are also important. Evidence has shown that as the health and status of women improve, population pressures become more manageable.

POPULATION GROWTH

Reduced rate of population growth in the United States and the world.

STATUS OF WOMEN

Increased educational opportunity for women; increased income equality for equivalent work.

UNINTENDED PREGNANCIES

Decreased number of unintended pregnancies in the United States.

TEEN PREGNANCIES

Decreased number of teenage pregnancies in the United States.

IMMIGRATION

Decreased number of illegal immigrants.

GOAL 9

INTERNATIONAL RESPONSIBILITY

Take a leadership role in the development and implementation of global sustainable development policies, standards of conduct, and trade and foreign policies, that further the achievement of sustainability.

FIGURE 9

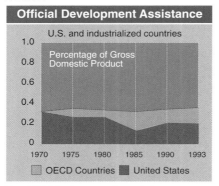

Official Development Assistance

U.S. and industrialized countries

Percentage of Gross Domestic Product

1.0
0.8
0.6
0.4
0.2
0

1970 1975 1980 1985 1990 1993

☐ OECD Countries ■ United States

NOTE: Official development assistance is the net amount of dispersed grants and concessional loans given by member countries of the Organization for Economic Cooperation and Development (OECD).

SOURCE: *Statistical Abstract of the United States 1994.*

INDICATORS OF PROGRESS

The actions taken by the United States have a significant effect on the world's environment, economy, and cultures. This nation has a tradition of global leadership and responsibility. It is important to continue this tradition. While indicators of global leadership apply to all sectors, the following ones focus on the role of the federal government.

INTERNATIONAL ASSISTANCE

Increased level of U.S. international assistance for sustainable development, including official development assistance (federal money dedicated to international aid for developing nations).

ENVIRONMENTAL ASSISTANCE

Increase in the U.S. contribution to the Global Environmental Facility and other environmentally targeted development aid.

ASSESSMENT OF PROGRESS

Development and use of new measures for assessing progress toward sustainable development in countries receiving U.S. assistance.

ENVIRONMENTAL TECHNOLOGY EXPORTS

Increased U.S. exports or transfers of cost-effective and environmentally sound technologies to developing countries.

RESEARCH LEADERSHIP

Increased levels of U.S. research on global environmental problems.

GOAL 10

EDUCATION

Ensure that all Americans have equal access to education and lifelong learning opportunities that will prepare them for meaningful work, a high quality of life, and an understanding of the concepts involved in sustainable development.

FIGURE 10

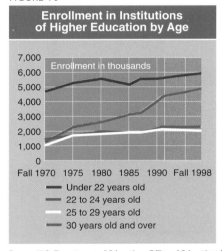

Enrollment in Institutions of Higher Education by Age

Enrollment in thousands

	Fall 1970	1975	1980	1985	1990	Fall 1998

- ▬ Under 22 years old
- ▬ 22 to 24 years old
- ▬ 25 to 29 years old
- ▬ 30 years old and over

SOURCE: U.S. Department of Education, Office of Educational Research and Improvement, *Digest of Education Statistics 1995* (Washington, D.C.: Government Printing Office, 1993).

INDICATORS OF PROGRESS

Education for sustainable development should be lifelong through integration into formal and nonformal education settings, including teacher education, continuing education, curriculum development, and worker training.

INFORMATION ACCESS

Increased number of communities with infrastructure in place that allows easy access to government information, public and private research, and community right-to-know documents.

CURRICULUM DEVELOPMENT

Increased number of curricula, materials, and training opportunities that teach the principles of sustainable development.

NATIONAL STANDARDS

Increased number of school systems that have adopted K-12 voluntary standards for learning about sustainable development similar to the standards developed under the National Goals 2000 initiative.

COMMUNITY PARTICIPATION

Increased number of school systems and communities with programs for lifelong learning through both formal and nonformal learning institutions.

NATIONAL ACHIEVEMENT

Improved skill performance of U.S. students as measured by standardized achievement tests.

GRADUATION RATES

Increased high school graduation rates and number of students going on to college or vocational training.

CHAPTER 2

BUILDING A NEW FRAMEWORK FOR A NEW CENTURY

Future progress requires that the United States broaden its commitment to environmental protection to embrace the essential components of sustainable development: environmental health, economic prosperity, and social equity and well-being. This means reforming the current system of environmental management and building a new and efficient framework based on performance, flexibility linked to accountability, extended product responsibility, tax and subsidy reform, and market incentives.

THE U.S. SYSTEM of environmental management, built largely since 1970, has dramatically improved the country's ability to protect public health and the natural environment. The air and water are cleaner, exposure to toxic wastes is lower, erosion of prime cropland has been reduced, and some wildlife species are back from the brink of extinction. Much still remains to be done, however, to continue these gains and address new environmental threats.

For the last 25 years, government has relied on command-and-control regulation as its primary tool for environmental management. In looking to the future, society needs to adopt a wider range of strategic environmental protection approaches that embrace the essential components of sustainable development: economic prosperity, environmental health, and social equity and well-being. The relationships among these components are clear. Sustained economic growth is dependent on a clean and healthy environment. Further, the ability of the economy to grow, create jobs, and increase overall well-being can suffer if environmental protection strategies deliver low results at a high cost. Resources for other economic and social needs will be diverted if strategies to achieve environmental goals are not designed to achieve results in the most cost-effective way. We, as a Council, have concluded that this will require the nation to develop a new framework for a new century.

[Certain] tools, approaches, and strategies . . . could result in more environmental protection, less economic cost, and . . . greater opportunity for the poor and disadvantaged.

There are a number of tools, approaches, and strategies that, if carefully tailored to different challenges, could result in more environmental protection, less economic cost, and — in some cases — greater opportunity for the poor and disadvantaged. It should be clear that market mechanisms are not the right solution for every problem, any more than technology-based standards are the right answer in all cases. The nation should create a new framework for integrating economic and environmental goals that lets all stakeholders take advantage of these opportunities and ensures that tools are applied to the right problem, in the right way, at the right time.

The experience of the last 25 years has yielded the following lessons, which would be wise to heed in developing a new framework to achieve the objectives of sustainable development:

- • • Economic, environmental, and social problems cannot be addressed in isolation. Economic prosperity, environmental quality, and social equity need to be pursued simultaneously.
- • • Science-based national standards that protect human health and the environment are the foundation of any effective system of environmental protection.
- • • The adversarial nature of the current system precludes solutions that become possible when potential adversaries cooperate and collaborate.

• • • Technology-based regulation can sometimes encourage technological innovation, but it can also stifle it; pollution prevention is better than pollution control.

• • • Enhanced flexibility for achieving environmental goals, coupled with strong compliance assurance mechanisms — including enforcement — can spur private sector innovation that will enhance environmental protection at a substantially lower cost both to individual firms and to society as a whole.

• • • Science, economics, and societal values should be considered in making decisions. Quality information is essential to sound decisionmaking.

• • • Many state governments have developed significant environmental management capacity. Indeed, many of the most creative and lasting solutions arise from collaborations involving federal, state, local, and tribal governments in places problems exist — from urban communities to watersheds.

Learning to use new approaches to achieve interrelated goals simultaneously will be an evolutionary process. It needs to build on the strengths and overcome the limitations of current economic and regulatory systems and recognize the interrelationships between economic and environmental policies. This will require pursuing change concurrently on two paths: making the existing regulatory system more efficient and more effective, and developing an alternative system of environmental management that uses innovative approaches. Besides improving the cost-effectiveness of the current system, the Council believes that the nation needs to develop policy tools that meet the following broad criteria:

• • • **Provide Greater Regulatory Flexibility With Accountability.** The regulatory system must give companies and communities greater operating flexibility, enabling them to reduce their costs significantly in exchange for achieving superior environmental performance. While allowing flexibility, the system must also require accountability to ensure that public health and the environment are protected.

• • • **Extend Product Responsibility.** A voluntary system of extended product responsibility can be adopted in which designers, producers, suppliers, users, and disposers accept responsibility for environmental effects through all phases of a product's life.

• • • **Make Greater Use of Market Forces.** Sustainable development objectives must harness market forces through policy tools, such as emissions trading deposit/refund systems and tax and subsidy reform. This approach can substantially influence the behavior of firms, governments, and individuals.

• • • **Use Intergovernmental Partnerships.** Federal, state, and tribal governments need to work together in partnership with local communities to develop place-based strategies that integrate economic development, environmental quality, and social policymaking with broad public involvement.

• • • **Encourage Environmental Technologies.** The economic and environmental management systems need to create an environment that encourages innovation and the development and use of technologies that will create jobs while reducing risks to human health and harm to the environment.

DEVELOPING A MORE COST-EFFECTIVE ENVIRONMENTAL MANAGEMENT SYSTEM BASED ON PERFORMANCE, FLEXIBILITY, AND ACCOUNTABILITY

In the past, government has relied mainly on regulatory approaches to managing environmental problems. Under this system, federal and state governments have set health-based standards, issued permits for discharges, and monitored and enforced standards set under each environmental statute. In some cases, regulations implementing these standards prescribe specific technologies to control pollution.

Over the years, the value and limits of this regulatory approach have become clear. There is no doubt that some regulations have encouraged innovation and compliance with environmental laws, resulting in substantial improvements in the protection of public health and the environment. But at other times, regulation has imposed unnecessary — and sometimes costly — administrative and technological burdens and discouraged technological innovations that can reduce costs while achieving environmental benefits beyond those realized by compliance. Moreover, it has frequently focused attention on cleanup and control remedies rather than on product or process redesign to prevent pollution.

Regulation . . . has frequently focused attention on cleanup and control remedies rather than on product or process redesign to prevent pollution.

Such concerns have contributed to a growing consensus that the existing regulatory system may be greatly improved by moving toward performance-based policies that encourage pollution prevention. Regulations that specify performance standards based on strong protection of health and the environment — but without mandating the means of compliance — give companies and communities flexibility to find the most cost-effective way to achieve environmental goals. In return for this flexibility, companies can pursue technological innovation that will result in superior environmental protection at far lower costs. But this flexibility must be coupled with accountability and enforcement to ensure that public health and the environment are safeguarded.

Just as the manufacturing sector has adopted a goal of zero defects, the nation can aspire to the ideal of a zero-waste society through more efficient use and recycling of natural resources in the economy and more efficient use of public and private financial resources in the regulatory system. The nation should pursue two paths in reforming environmental regulation. The first is to improve the efficiency and effectiveness of the current environmental management system. The second is to develop and test innovative approaches and create a new alternative environmental management system that achieves more protection at a lower cost. To help achieve this, the administrator of the U.S. Environmental Protection Agency (EPA), working in partnership with other federal agencies and other stakeholders, should have the authority to make decisions that will achieve environmental goals efficiently and effectively.

Although moving away from a one-size-fits-all approach will reduce costs to the private sector, creating an optional system could increase administrative and policy burdens on federal agencies, at least in the short term. Like clothing, custom-tailored environmental management may cost the public sector more to deliver than the off-the-rack variety. The new alternative system is designed to reduce aggregate costs to society, but it will require both industry and government to use new skills and resources, especially at the beginning. Negotiating facility-by-facility agreements is labor-intensive compared to administering permit compliance checklists. Developing facility-specific performance measures to ensure business accountability for negotiated goals is more expensive than enforcing uniform standards. Convening stakeholder workshops to reach agreeable environmental goals requires additional travel and staff time. The system would also require a farsighted investment posture on the part of businesses seeking to break out of prescribed solutions to create their own. Nonetheless, the improved environmental protection system is designed to reduce total costs to the private and public sectors over time and will improve the nation's overall economic performance.

Partnerships and collaborative decisionmaking must be encouraged and must involve all levels of government, businesses, nongovernmental organizations, community groups, and the public at large. Initiatives are needed to verify that increased operational flexibility on a facilitywide basis can produce environmental performance superior to the current system while greatly reducing costs. To help ensure accountability, demonstrations also are needed to increase public involvement and access to information. The new system should facilitate voluntary initiatives that encourage businesses and consumers to assume responsibility for their actions. At the same time, the regulatory system must continue to provide a safety net of public health and environmental protection by guaranteeing compliance with basic standards.

Movement toward a performance-based system will be aided by public-private partnerships promoting the research, development, and application of cost-effective technologies and practices. Continued, long-term investment in technology will help ensure U.S. competitiveness and leadership in global technology markets. New manufacturing technologies and processes can lower material and energy use while reducing or eliminating waste streams. Focusing efforts to develop cleaner and more efficient products for domestic and overseas markets will help base U.S. economic growth on the concept of better — rather than just more — products and processes.

THE POLLUTION PREVENTION PILOT PROJECT

How can companies save money and cut down on waste and pollution? What are the public policy changes that would help companies innovate to increase their economic and environmental efficiency?

These questions brought together a group of experts from industry and the environmental community to learn how money-saving pollution prevention happens at the facility level. The Pollution Prevention Pilot Project (4P) is led by a core group from the Natural Resources Defense Council (NRDC), Amoco Petroleum, The Dow Chemical Company, Monsanto Company, Rayonier, and the New Jersey Department of Environmental Protection.

With a shared industry-environmentalist perspective, the core group, facility staff, and an experienced pollution prevention consultant have begun to identify opportunities to cut production and environmental costs while reducing and preventing pollution at two chemical manufacturing facilities — a Dow Chemical plant in La Porte, Texas, and a Monsanto plant in Pensacola, Florida. Early results show that major cost savings and significant environmental improvements can be achieved by looking for creative ways to address environmental issues.

Through site-specific work, the group is exploring what internal, external, or regulatory barriers may have kept the plants involved from already practicing cost-saving pollution prevention. Later, the group will try to craft policy proposals to spur more economically and environmentally sound innovation.

"The 4P initiative demonstrates that industry and the environmental community can work together for success — enhanced environmental improvements and economic savings. This is an excellent example of how innovative partnerships can yield more through our collective efforts than each could accomplish alone," says David Buzzelli, vice president and corporate director of Dow Chemical, and co-chair of the President's Council on Sustainable Development.

Adds John Adams, executive director of NRDC and a Council member, "What is exciting about this project is that it can produce tremendous environmental benefits by tapping the traditional strength of business — its ability to build a better mousetrap, to find better and more efficient ways of producing a product."

POLICY RECOMMENDATION 2

. . . .

ALTERNATIVE PERFORMANCE-BASED MANAGEMENT SYSTEM

(continued)

ACTION 3. EPA and state agencies should accelerate efforts to conduct a series of demonstration projects to gain experience with policy tools and innovative approaches that could serve as the basis for an alternative environmental management system. They should be to work with all interested parties to tailor compliance terms of demonstrations that make a credible commitment to going beyond existing standards. For example, longer compliance periods might be considered for demonstrations that are designed to achieve superior protection, but this flexibility could be coupled with interim reporting requirements. Alternatively, demonstrations that focus on environmental performance of an entire facility rather than on separate air, water, and soil requirements might stipulate that environmental gains for an entire facility exceed what would have been achieved through source-by-source or medium-specific regulations. These provisions would help ensure that all parties operate in good faith — an essential element of creating trust.

The federal government, working with the private sector and nongovernmental organizations, should review and evaluate the lessons learned from the demonstration projects. Based on the success of the first round of demonstration projects, a second set of projects should be selected within two years.

ACTION 4. National laboratories and federal research agencies should be directed to conduct research necessary to help develop, test, and verify the scientific basis of technologies and practices to move toward the ideal of a zero-waste society. This research would help ensure that over time the new system would reflect improved scientific information and understanding. Research agencies should identify health risks, monitor trends and environmental conditions, and inform decision-makers of emerging environmental challenges. National laboratories should have the resources they need to help identify opportunities for public-private technology partnerships and be available to evaluate the effectiveness of new technologies and practices in attaining environmental goals at lower cost.

REGULATORY FLEXIBILITY AND ACCOUNTABILITY IN ACTION

Collaboration and experimentation both inside and outside the government and between government and private enterprise are leading to more effective ways of meeting environmental goals while reducing costs. Through the Common Sense Initiative, the U.S. Environmental Protection Agency (EPA) has convened consensus-oriented teams to look for opportunities to turn complicated and inconsistent environmental regulations into comprehensive sector-specific strategies for environmental protection.

Six major industries are the focus of the project's first phase: automobile manufacturing, computers and electronics, iron and steel, metal finishing, petroleum refining, and printing. These major industries account for more than 11 percent of the gross domestic product, employ nearly 4 million people, and generate a significant portion of the toxic releases reported. Representatives from federal, state, and local governments; community-based and national environmental groups; environmental justice groups; labor; and industry are examining the full range of environmental requirements affecting the six pilot industries. Teams are working to find cleaner, cheaper, smarter approaches in the areas of regulation, reporting, compliance, permitting, and environmental technology — emphasizing pollution prevention instead of end-of-pipe controls.

Project XL is a second example of regulatory flexibility and accountability in action, this time looking at specific facilities rather than specific industries. Six companies — Intel Corporation; Anheuser Busch Companies; HADCO Corporation; Merck & Co., Inc.; AT&T Microelectronics; and 3M Corporation — and two government agencies — California's South Coast Air Quality Management District and the Minnesota Pollution Control Agency — will participate in the first phase of the Project XL initiative. Denoting Excellence and Leadership, Project XL allows selected businesses and communities to experiment with innovative and flexible strategies to achieve greater environmental results, while providing regulatory flexibility and maintaining accountability. For example, Intel will enter into a contract with EPA and the Arizona Department of Environmental Quality for its new facility in Chandler, Arizona. As proposed, the company will agree to achieve better environmental results than are currently required for air, land, and water pollution. For their part, regulators will grant Intel more regulatory flexibility and expedited permitting procedures, making it easier for the company to meet the higher environmental goals.[2]

On November 3, 1995, President Bill Clinton announced the selection of Intel and the other five firms chosen for the first phase of Project XL: "To industry, Project XL shows that protecting the health and safety of our citizens doesn't have to come at the expense of a bottom line. And to those in the environmental community, XL shows that strengthening the economy doesn't have to come at the expense of the air we breathe, the food we eat, the water we drink."

POWER, LEG ROOM, AND 80 MILES TO THE GALLON

Early in the next century, customers could have an exciting new option when they shop for a new automobile. They may be able to purchase cars that achieve up to 80 miles to the gallon, are mostly recyclable, accelerate from 0 to 60 miles per hour in 12 seconds, comfortably hold six passengers, meet all safety and emissions requirements, and cost about the same as comparably sized cars on the showroom floor.

This new generation of car could represent more than a breakthrough in fuel efficiency and design. It would also represent a breakthrough in cooperation among competing automobile manufacturers and among the automobile industry, suppliers, universities, other small and large businesses, and the U.S. government.

On September 29, 1993, Vice President Al Gore and the chief executive officers of the Ford Motor Company, Chrysler Corporation, and General Motors Corporation announced a historic Partnership for a New Generation of Vehicles. The partnership has three objectives: to improve national competitiveness in manufacturing, to promote commercially viable near-term innovation, and to develop a vehicle that is up to three times more efficient than today's comparable vehicle. Achieving this level of fuel economy would stretch the boundaries of technical capability. Underlying these goals is yet another challenge: affordability.

Vice President Gore, meeting with members of the President's Council on Sustainable Development, received an update on the partnership effort during a January 1995 visit to Chattanooga, Tennessee. "By the end of 1997, we will narrow the technology focus. By 2000, we will have a concept vehicle. And by the year 2004, we will have a production prototype," declared a representative of the partnership. "This is not just about jobs," he added. "It is not just about technology. It is not just about the environment. It is also about a new process of working together, for both industry and government, in ways that have not been attempted before."

ADOPTING EXTENDED PRODUCT RESPONSIBILITY

While environmental programs that focus on a point in the product chain have resulted in resource conservation and pollution prevention, further advances will only be incremental ones as long as the approach taken continues to separate all stages of economic activity, including product design, manufacture, use, and disposal. For example, when looking to reduce air emissions of a particular chemical associated with a product, the production plant is often not the only place to examine. Sometimes, more cost-effective and larger reductions can be found by analyzing emissions from transporting and distributing the product. A life-cycle approach captures the upstream environmental effects associated with raw material selection and use and effects from production processes and product distribution. It also reflects downstream effects associated with product use, recycling, and disposal. Life-cycle approaches can yield better environmental results at lower cost.

Creating an innovative system of extended product responsibility would improve the current fragmented approach to waste reduction, resource conservation, and pollution prevention.

Extended product responsibility is an emerging principle that uses this life-cycle approach to identify strategic opportunities for pollution prevention and resource conservation. It also addresses the underlying influence of consumer needs and preferences, government procurement, and the role played by those in the chain of production and distribution. Under the principle of extended product responsibility, manufacturers, suppliers, users, and disposers of products share responsibility for the environmental effects of products and waste streams.

Creating an innovative system of extended product responsibility would improve the current fragmented approach to waste reduction, resource conservation, and pollution prevention. When there are missing links in the chain of responsibility, waste and inefficiency result. Communities bear the greatest burden for the disposal of hazardous products. Similarly, decisions made upstream in the chain by suppliers can reduce a manufacturer's emissions and wastes and improve profitability. Sharing responsibility implies not only understanding and communicating the environmental effects of product development but also acting collectively to reduce them. By using a mix of regulatory and other incentives, information, education, and institutional support, this new system would encourage individuals, government, and corporations to recognize, understand, and act on the basis of their responsibility to advance sustainable development objectives. Further, government agencies — the nation's largest consumers — can use their market leverage to encourage U.S. manufacturers to increase the efficiency of materials use. Purchasing specifications can give manufacturers strong incentives to create products that result in fewer environmental effects while maintaining similar product performance.

This policy recommendation constitutes a challenge to the American people to develop models of shared responsibility and demonstrate how these models can be put into effect across the country and throughout the world. For example, liability regimes must be consistent with any shifts of product responsibility. A series of demonstration projects that illustrate new models of shared responsibility throughout different product systems could provide valuable experience with extended product responsibility. While extended product responsibility should constitute a national priority, actions of states and localities are integral to its success. Ultimately, the Council believes that sharing responsibility for environmental effects would transform the marketplace into one driven by:

- More efficient use of resources;
- Cleaner products and technologies;
- More efficient and more competitive manufacturing;
- Safer storage, shipping, and handling of materials;
- Improved relations between communities and companies;
- Improved recycling and recovery; and
- Responsible consumer choices.

FIGURE 11

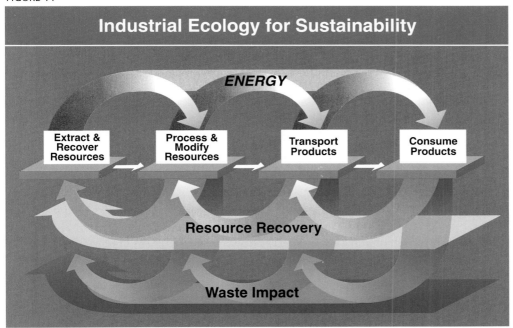

NOTES: Industrial ecology is the study of a closed loop in which resources and energy flow into production processes, and excess materials are put back into the loop so that little or no waste is generated. Products used by consumers flow back into production loops through recycling to recover resources. Ideally, the loops are closed within a factory, among industries in a region, and within national and global economies.

SOURCE: Office of Science and Technology Policy, *Technology for a Sustainable Future* (Washington, D.C., 1994).

POLICY RECOMMENDATION 3

EXTENDED PRODUCT RESPONSIBILITY

Adopt a voluntary system that ensures responsibility for the environmental effects throughout a product's life cycle by all those involved in the life cycle. The greatest opportunity for extended product responsibility rests with those throughout the commerce chain — designers, suppliers, manufacturers, distributors, users, and disposers — that are in a position to practice resource conservation and pollution prevention at lower cost.

ACTION 1. Companies, trade associations, wholesalers, retailers, consumer groups, and other private sector parties can develop models of shared product responsibility. Private sector parties should solicit the participation of government and environmental representatives in developing voluntary product responsibility models or demonstration project proposals. Each demonstration project proposal should identify critical links in the product chain, opportunities for significant improvements, and key participants that need to be involved to prevent pollution or conserve resources within each product system under consideration.

ACTION 2. A joint committee involving the private and nonprofit sectors should recommend to the President individuals to be appointed to a Product Responsibility Panel to review and select demonstration projects, help identify appropriate participants, and provide advice on the execution of the demonstration projects themselves. Demonstrations should include companion training and educational programs to communicate the objectives of the demonstrations and principles of extended product responsibility. The Product Responsibility Panel should help identify means of conducting effective monitoring, evaluation, and analysis of the projects' progress and possible links with other sustainable development initiatives. It should also help coordinate sound economic and environmental analyses to assist in transferring the lessons from local demonstration projects to regional and national policies. The panel should have a balanced representation of stakeholders with interests in the life cycle of a product, including its supply, procurement, consumption, and disposal. By immediately identifying product categories for demonstration projects, U.S. industry, in cooperation with government agencies and the environmental community, could begin to carry out the new models of shared responsibility to produce rapid and measurable results. Necessary measures to protect against the extension of product liability would encourage the voluntary assumption of responsibility by businesses.

ACTION 3. Following evaluation of the projects, the federal government, private companies, and individuals should voluntarily adopt practices and policies that have been successfully demonstrated to carry out extended product responsibility on a regional and national scale. The Product Responsibility Panel should recommend any legislative changes needed to remove barriers to extending product responsibility. The procurement policies of federal, state, local, and tribal governments should reflect preferences for resulting cost-effective, environmentally superior products.

FROM THE TOP OF A MOUNTAIN
TO THE HEART OF THE CITY

Ever wonder what happens to those recycled plastic soda bottles? Just take a walk along a mountain trail on a crisp autumn day. Many of the brightly clad hikers will be sporting jackets that were once soda bottles. Pile jackets, produced from petroleum-based fibers, have been worn for over two decades; today, many are made from recycled plastic bottles.

One producer of the recycled fabric is Malden Mills, a century-old business located in the Lawrence/Methuen area of Massachusetts. Malden estimates that in 1995 about 20 percent of the pile it manufactures will come from recycled soda bottles. With each jacket using around 20 bottles, more than 140 million bottles each year will be in clothing rather than in landfills. Along with using 60 times less new plastic, recycled fibers discharge 17 times fewer pollutants, six times less sulfur dioxide, and four times less carbon dioxide.

"The whole notion of product stewardship — minimizing waste, water use, energy use, chemical use — as well as how we work with our customers and suppliers is a fundamental principle of our company," says Walter Bickford, Malden's environmental manager. "You need to encourage top-down and bottom-up support within the corporation and along each step in the supply chain."

One of Malden's customers, Patagonia, an outdoor clothing company, is also wrestling with the concept of corporate stewardship. Its founder, Yvon Chouinard, discusses his concerns in the book Sacred Trusts. "Other than shutting down the doors and giving up, what Patagonia can do is to constantly assess what we are doing. With education comes choices, and we can continue to work toward reducing the damage we do. In this process, we will face tough questions that have no clear-cut answers. Should we add a bit of synthetic fiber in a cotton fabric if it makes a pair of pants last twice as long? Which is better to use — toxic chemical dyes or natural dyes that are less colorfast and will fade?"[3]

For businesses like Malden and Patagonia, stewardship extends beyond products and includes a strong commitment to the communities in which they are located. Malden's hometown of Lawrence is a struggling New England mill town where the population is half its post-World War II peak of 90,000. Starting in the late 1950s, it faced a population exodus as textile firms migrated South or overseas. By the 1980s, acres of downtown Lawrence were a vast wasteland of abandoned buildings. Malden, which employs 2,500 workers at its Lawrence factory, is now the city's largest employer and has a strong influence over the health of its economy.

"Stewardship ultimately comes back to growth policy and land use planning," says Bickford. "For us, that means sticking with a depressed and crime-ridden city. It means renovating our turn-of-the-century brick factory that lies in the heart of that city. It means a workforce that is 70 percent minority, paid union wages. It means educating ourselves, our employees, and the community. In sum, it means achieving product excellence with social responsibility."

[Before our report went to press, Malden Mills was struck by a tragic fire which destroyed much of the factory. Malden's president, Aaron Feuerstein, recently announced that the company plans to rebuild the plant on the same location as soon as possible.]

TOOLS FOR EXTENDED PRODUCT RESPONSIBILITY

A variety of tools can help make extended product responsibility a reality. Some, like labeling programs, inform consumers. Others, like product fees, put a value on environmental impact. All help decisionmakers recognize and respond to opportunities to change. These tools may focus on individual actions or reflect coordination among many participants in the chain of commerce. The tools used for a particular product category should be designed to achieve the desired change at the most appropriate links in the chain, and, where possible, by voluntary action. Following are examples of these tools.

Product Stewardship Programs and Public-Private Partnerships: Stewardship programs typically deal with the downstream environmental and safety aspects of product use. Many companies and organizations already have voluntary programs of this nature. Examples include the U.S. Environmental Protection Agency's Green Programs such as the Energy Star[R] initiatives; Chemical Manufacturers Association's Responsible Care[R] program; Environmental Defense Fund/McDonald's partnership; and initiatives by the Business Council for Sustainable Development, Coalition for Environmentally Responsible Economies, International Standards Organization, National Association of Chemical Distributors, and Synthetic Organic Chemical Manufacturers Association.

Take Back, Buy Back, Leasing, or Reuse/Recycling: Under take-back or buy-back systems, products, packaging, or waste materials are returned to their source for reuse, recycling, treatment, or safe disposal. This mitigates downstream environmental effects and permits recovery of valuable materials. Take-back programs are not appropriate for all product categories, such as those that are extremely complex or where recycling infrastructure already exists, but there are many valid applications. Under leasing systems, ownership of materials or products is never transferred, thus encouraging manufacturers to close material flow loops and extend product life. Reuse or recycling by other manufacturers also closes material flow loops.

Education, Information, or Training: Purchasers and users can be given information to facilitate informed environmental decisions. Information can be made available through labeling, product literature, and certification programs. What is important is a continuous flow of information from the designer to the manufacturer, to the user, and back to the designer.

Government Subsidies, Tax Credits, and Procurement Preference: Direct subsidies or tax credits can encourage sustainable processes and products. Because a national priority is usually the justification for a subsidy or tax credit, these tools should not conflict with the goals of sustainability and should be revenue neutral. Federal, state, local, and tribal governments can exert influence in the marketplace through their purchase specifications for environmentally superior products.

Taxes/Fees or Deposit/Refund Systems: Taxes and fees can add the value of environmental effects to the costs of materials and products, making them relatively less preferable in the marketplace. Taxes and fees can also be used to shift the cost of waste management to the waste generator. Examples include taxes on automobile tires and variable pricing for household wastes.

RESPONSIBLE CARE*

When the Vista Chemical Company expanded its Lake Charles, Louisiana, plant's ethylene unit, community members expressed concern about high flames coming out of a stack. "Our neighbors were afraid of the high flames and unhappy about the vibration and noise caused by the flares," according to Nancy Tower, community relations coordinator at the Lake Charles plant. "That's why we held assembly meetings at local schools, distributed information to the media, and sent mailers out informing the community about the flare's role as a safety and control device." Ultimately, the company decided that the only way to really address community concern was to purchase a flare tip to reduce the noise. Tower notes, "This is an example of the public outreach that we are committed to and the dialogue that Responsible Care encourages."

Responsible Care is an initiative that provides the ethical framework within which member and partner companies of the Chemical Manufacturers Association (CMA) operate. It was adopted in 1988 and is continually subject to critical appraisal with an eye toward improved implementation. All CMA members and partners pledge to abide by 10 underlying principles, which include recognizing and responding to community concerns about chemicals and plant operations; developing and producing chemicals that can be manufactured, transported, and disposed of safely; making health, safety, and environmental considerations a planning priority; reporting promptly on health or environmental hazards and recommending protective measures; pursuing relevant research and communications activities; and participating with government and others in creating responsible laws, regulations, and standards to safeguard the community, workplace, and environment. A public advisory panel composed of individuals from the public and private sectors meets four times a year and helps CMA identify public concerns and decide how to respond to them, reviews Responsible Care's codes of management practices, and evaluates other features of the initiative.

In sum, says Fred Webber, president of CMA, "Through Responsible Care, the chemical industry has taken a significant step toward satisfying the public's desire for both useful products and a safe and clean environment. The chemical industry's commitment to following through on performance improvement is unprecedented. In my opinion, Responsible Care is more than a good initiative — it's the industry's franchise to operate."

*Responsible Care[R] is a registered trademark of the Chemical Manufacturers Association.

GREATER USE OF MARKET FORCES

In the American economic system, the marketplace plays a central role in guiding what people produce, how they produce it, and what they consume. The choices and decisions made by millions of consumers and firms determine prices for the wide range of goods and services that constitute the national economy. The marketplace's power to produce desired goods and services at the lowest cost possible is driven by the price signals that result from this decentralized decision process.

Despite the nation's commitment to a free market economic system, governmental policy substantially influences the workings of the marketplace. For example, tax levels on different products and activities lower or raise their market prices and artificially encourage or discourage their use. Some government subsidy programs encourage activities that result in economic inefficiency as well as destructive use of resources. At other times, government tax and spending subsidy programs may be essential if the short-term rewards of the marketplace do not coincide with the long-term goals of the nation. To ignore the importance of economic policy is to miss opportunities to encourage economic, environmental, and equity goals.

To improve environmental performance, the design of environmental and natural resource programs should take advantage of the positive role the marketplace can play once environmental goals and market signals are aligned. Current policies generally do not use the power of the marketplace, and at present, some environmental costs in the product chain may be shifted to society at large, rather than be fully reflected in the product price. The cost of air, soil, and water pollution associated with materials and energy used in production as well as the expense to local communities for product disposal are two examples of costs not typically included in a product price. But if these types of costs are reflected in the price of a product, the marketplace sends an important signal. All other things being equal, consumers generally will purchase the lower priced product, creating an important incentive for a company to reconsider how it makes a product. Increasing the use of market forces can create opportunities to achieve natural resource and environmental goals in the most cost-effective way possible by encouraging the innovation that flows from a competitive economic system.

Examples of market incentive strategies include greater use of systems that allow regulated firms to buy and sell emissions reductions rather than more traditional pollution control approaches, reform of governmental tax and spending policies, and more comprehensive measures of economic performance.[4]

PRESERVING THE LONG ISLAND PINE BARRENS

For more than 20 years, developers, environmentalists, and local government officials in Suffolk County, New York, waged a costly and emotionally charged battle over the Pine Barrens, a 100,000-acre expanse of rare pitch pines and scrub oak forest located on Long Island. In addition to being valued natural habitat, the Pine Barrens rest atop a vast underground aquifer that provides water for the residents of Suffolk County, one of the most densely populated counties in the nation. The prolonged and intense conflict over the Pine Barrens eventually culminated in a lawsuit brought by the Long Island Pine Barrens Society.

In 1993, weary of litigation and stung by a real estate recession, the parties to the dispute and other stakeholders, aided by the Suffolk County Water Authority, joined together to help the state legislature draft a bill that led to the creation of the Pine Barrens Commission. The commission promotes a distinctive management plan for the region, which, except in special hardship cases, will prohibit further development in a 52,500-acre core preservation area, of which 14,000 acres are privately owned, and will foster efficient, compact development in a surrounding 47,500-acre growth area and outside the central Pine Barrens altogether. It will achieve this not only through outright purchase of some land but through an innovative market-oriented method to preserve vital areas.

Under the plan, landowners in the core area whose property is not acquired outright but who cannot build on it, can sell their development rights for use in outlying areas that are suitable for higher density development than local zoning currently allows. The plan has identified three types of receiving areas: areas where residential development may increase modestly, areas where commercial density may increase, and planned development districts where densities may increase substantially. The result is a program that offers a cost-effective and equitable way to preserve land with the potential to improve the future shape of communities on the periphery of the Pine Barrens.

Across the United States, communities are struggling to save ecologically important areas while also allowing for growth and development. The use of transfer of development rights helps address this challenge by harnessing market incentives to allow developers, environmentalists, and local citizens to implement new methods for long-term community planning.

Tax Shift and Subsidy Reform

It became increasingly apparent as several of the Council's task forces grappled with various aspects of sustainable development that tax policy is an important consideration in formulating strategies for achieving the desired goals.

The Council believes a tax system should be designed to raise sufficient revenues without discouraging capital formation, job creation, environmental improvement, and social equity. Currently, the federal government raises more than $1 trillion per year, predominantly (nearly 90 percent) by taxing wages and personal and corporate income.[5] And since tax policies influence individual and institutional investment patterns and consumption decisions, the Council believes that an effective use of the tax system could be a powerful tool in meeting the challenges of sustainable development. Council members wrestled with the question of whether these challenges could be met, in part, by shifting some of the nation's taxes to activities and forms of consumption that are economically bad for society — inefficiency, waste, and pollution — and away from those that are economically good — employment, income, and savings and investment.

Ideally, a tax system that supports the recommendations of the Council would promote economic growth and jobs in a socially equitable manner, while discouraging pollution and other forms of inefficiency. The Council believes substantial progress in reaching these objectives can be made through revenue-neutral system improvements — changes that shift the ways revenues are raised without increasing overall tax obligations. In addition to revenue neutrality, tax reform efforts must be guided by the following criteria:

• • • Tax policy must ensure that individuals and families at different income levels are treated as fairly as possible. We, as a Council, strongly believe that taxes should not place a disproportionate burden on lower income individuals and families, and we recognize the limitation of some options — such as the value-added tax or a national sales tax — in meeting this criterion. Federal tax policy must address social equity to be consistent with the goals of sustainable development.

• • • The tax system must promote savings and investment, employment, and economic growth. The Council is firmly convinced that any tax shift should encourage savings, private investment, and job creation.

• • • Tax-based policy should also be more skillfully employed to provide for enhanced environmental performance. While there was strong support among many of the Council members to shift tax policy from "taxing goods to taxing bads," there was no consensus regarding any of the specific policy options discussed. However, the Council acknowledged that there is sufficient merit to market mechanisms, such as pollution taxes and taxes on consumption, to warrant further evaluation. Moreover, the Council did agree that any tax shift needs to be done gradually, will not obviate the need for legally enforceable environmental standards or agreements, and should be designed to increase the efficiency of national efforts to improve environmental quality.

Although special tax, spending, and credit provisions may have been economically justified at some time in the nation's development, they may no longer be serving their original purposes and instead may have unintended side effects that run counter to national economic and environmental objectives.

In addition to recognizing the need for alignment of tax policy with the goals of sustainable development, the Council emphasized the need to examine the practical effects of various kinds of subsidies, some of which are obvious and appear to conflict with the Council's goals. As this nation moves toward a more sustainable society, the Council believes that it is absolutely essential to scrutinize existing subsidies and to determine their efficiency in advancing the goals of sustainable development.

POLICY RECOMMENDATION 4

SHIFT IN TAX POLICIES

Begin the long-term process of shifting to tax policies that — without increasing overall tax burdens — encourage employment and economic opportunity while discouraging environmentally damaging production and consumption decisions.

POLICY RECOMMENDATION 5

SUBSIDY REFORM

Eliminate government subsidies that encourage activities inconsistent with economic, environmental, and social goals.

ACTION 1. A national commission should be established to review the effect of federal tax and subsidy policies on the goals of sustainable development. The commission would have two major responsibilities. First, it should conduct an explicit assessment of alternative tax policies and, in particular, should assess opportunities for increased use of pollution taxes while reducing reliance on more traditional income taxes. The commission should make recommendations to the President and Congress on tax reform initiatives that are consistent with the goals of economic prosperity, a healthy environment, and social equity.

Second, the commission should review all existing tax and spending subsidies to determine if there remains a national need to continue individual subsidies. The commission should recommend to the President a list of subsidies that fail to meet this test and should be phased out or rapidly eliminated. Any remaining subsidies should be made subject to a sunset or review clause that would require the appropriate government agency to ensure on a regular basis that these subsidies are not inconsistent with national sustainable development goals; otherwise they would be eliminated.

Unlike the tax reform proposal above, subsidies have been the subject of analysis and debate and their likely economic, environmental, and equity effects are relatively well-known. Proposals to reform subsidies have been prevented in the past by intractable political barriers that have proven very difficult to overcome. Hence, the commission should also evaluate alternative mechanisms for addressing these political hurdles. Modifications to the U.S. Tax Code or the elimination of subsidies would result in short-term dislocations, but would provide long-term benefits for the nation as a whole. The commission should evaluate and act on remedial or preventive steps to mitigate any short-term effects.

The commission should also recommend specific criteria for use by the executive branch and Congress in evaluating proposed subsidies to ensure compatibility with the goals of sustainable development.

Nontax Market Incentives

Federal, state, and local government efforts to protect the nation's natural resources and enhance environmental quality have a long way to go in tapping market-based incentives that could yield substantial environmental and economic benefits. Market incentives can take advantage of consumer and producer creativity and entrepreneurship to find solutions that are cleaner, cheaper, and more efficient.

Market incentives offer potential benefits for existing environmental and natural resource programs as well as new ones. For example, greater use of emissions trading initiatives, such as the sulfur dioxide trading system authorized under the current Clean Air Act, could enhance progress toward meeting and maintaining national air quality goals. This program assigns pollution targets to firms but then permits them to sell excess reductions, called allowances, to others. Firms with high pollution control costs can buy reductions from firms that were able to make greater reductions at lower costs, creating economic incentives to find the least expensive way to comply with regulations and rewarding companies that have achieved superior environmental performance. These economic incentives to reduce pollution also drive innovations and the development of cleaner and more efficient technologies. There are, in fact, a wide range of economic tools and instruments for environmental and natural resource protection. All share the common characteristic of creating flexibility and incentives for firms and consumers to find the best way to achieve the goals of sustainable development.

At the same time, however, it is important to recognize that market incentives are not an effective way to deal with all environmental threats. Such is the case with human exposure to highly toxic chemicals. Many environmental problems may still require specific rules and regulations to effect strict compliance and ensure protection of public health and the environment.

ENERGY AND SUSTAINABLE DEVELOPMENT

Decisions on energy production, distribution, and use can have important effects on the U.S. and global environment, the prices of most basic goods and services, international competitiveness, and national and economic security. Changes in technology and economic behavior offer an effective way to reduce the environmental and social burden associated with energy production and use. Cost-effective investments in energy efficiency, for example, lead to economic, environmental, and equity benefits by reducing energy costs and environmental effects. The energy sector and individual citizens can strive to improve the economic and environmental performance of energy use to enhance national competitiveness and social well-being.

It is important to recognize the global context of energy issues in shaping strategies for the future. If people in developing countries follow U.S. patterns of development, consume similar amounts of resources, and generate as much pollution, they will reinforce many unsustainable trends and undermine global progress in reducing environmental problems. Solutions and innovations developed for challenges in the United States can be adapted to conditions in developing countries to help them achieve their economic, environmental, and equity aspirations.

A number of the Council's policy recommendations would remove institutional, economic, and regulatory barriers that prevent progress toward achieving sustainable development in the energy sector. For example, the increased regulatory flexibility envisioned by the Council under an alternative performance-based management system would encourage energy efficiency as a method of pollution prevention. For many industries, introduction of innovative technologies that prevent pollution and lower compliance costs typically decreases energy consumption. The industries that produce the most pollution and incur the highest abatement costs — chemicals, petroleum refining, pulp and paper, and primary metals — also consume the most energy.[6] Successful research and development aimed at pollution prevention and waste minimization would reduce pollution remediation costs as well as consumption of energy and raw materials. Federal research and development technology partnerships are catalysts for innovation and can also create important economic incentives as part of an alternative performance-based management system.

Other policy recommendations that would help foster progress in the energy sector include shifting tax policies, reforming subsidies, and making greater use of market incentives as discussed earlier in this chapter. Progress in this area can be gauged using the following indicators:

• • • **Energy Use:** Reduction in the amount of energy consumed per dollar of gross domestic product.

• • • **Renewable Energy:** Increase in the share of renewable energy use in the U.S. energy supply.

• • • **Electricity Efficiency:** Increase in the average efficiency of electricity generation.

• • • **Greenhouse Gas Emissions:** Reduction in U.S. emissions of greenhouse gases due to human activity and a continued downward trend in other regulated pollutants.

POLICY RECOMMENDATION 6

USE OF MARKET INCENTIVES

Make greater use of market incentives as part of an overall environmental management system to achieve environmental and natural resource management objectives, whenever feasible. This system must provide for verification, accountability, and the means to ensure that national standards are met or exceeded.

ACTION 1. Federal and state governments should build on existing programs to design and carry out a system that allows the buying and selling of emissions reductions guaranteeing permanent overall reductions. Such systems should be appropriate to the environmental problems being addressed and local conditions. If applied appropriately, this approach would reduce the costs of meeting air and water quality standards without compromising human and environmental health.

ACTION 2. The federal government should work with the private sector and nonprofit groups to identify cost-effective opportunities to reuse and recycle materials. For example, federal, state, local, and tribal governments should use such information to design procurement policies to encourage new markets for recycled materials that will create jobs.

ACTION 3. States could develop incentives for energy-efficiency investments during the transition from highly regulated to more competitive electricity market forces to create a decentralized approach to investments in energy efficiency.

Energy efficiency is a primary tool of sustainability because it can help achieve the interdependent objectives of improving the economy, increasing equity, and reducing environmental costs. Despite the substantial efficiency gains of the past 20 years, consumers and industry can still save energy cost-effectively by using newer technologies and improved practices. Many of the least affluent in society have not yet reaped the economic gains from energy efficiency because of lack of financial resources and access to technology. And because current patterns of energy production exact a toll on the environment, energy efficiency can directly reduce environmental effects.

Over the past two decades, energy markets have become more competitive and direct governmental influence has waned. This is an evolution that has brought significant benefits for consumers and contributed to more efficient energy use. For example, the natural gas and electricity markets have moved from being completely regulated to being partially regulated with the introduction of new competitive forces. However, this transition to increased competition needs to be managed with efficiency and the environment in mind. Specifically, many analysts question whether even the best energy conservation programs currently in place will survive the transition to more competitive markets. Also unclear is the extent to which businesses will take advantage of opportunities in this area and

POLICY RECOMMENDATION 6

USE OF MARKET INCENTIVES

(continued)

respond with innovative approaches to replace traditional demand-side conservation programs. Energy efficiency should continue to be emphasized during the period of transition and beyond.

One approach would be to replace the existing patchwork of utility-sponsored conservation programs with temporary market-based approaches. Under this concept, states would place a small fee on all electricity users. The revenue collected would be placed into an energy efficiency fund awarded to electricity suppliers that compete for the opportunity to install cost-effective energy-saving equipment at a partially defrayed cost. The competition for projects would largely replace traditional bureaucratic programs with an active market in energy efficiency.

It is clear that residential, commercial, and small manufacturing customers, for example, that do not already engage in extensive demand-side conservation efforts would benefit from programs of this type. However, many large facilities that may be subject to global competition already make significant investments in energy efficiency as a business mainstay. In these cases, incentive programs involving surcharges may not be warranted.

ACTION 4. Congress should enact legislation to remove provisions in current laws prohibiting state and local governments from developing market-based transportation management strategies that more fully reflect travel costs. The U.S. Department of Transportation should encourage states and manufacturers to work together to standardize technology specifications to enable communities interested in doing so to adopt common standards for electronic road and parking pricing technologies.

States and localities that choose to use these market tools should apply the revenues to offset cuts in nontransportation taxes and to enhance the public transit and transportation systems, maintenance, and services. The revenues should also help finance toll discounts, exemptions, and/or rebates for low-income commuters who need to use the roads to travel to jobs during times of the day when tolls are collected. All levels of government should consider offering funding bonuses to areas that implement road user fees more fully. Bonuses should be available to states or regions that achieve measurable improvements in reducing transportation-related pollution, energy consumption, or vehicle miles traveled.

BUILDING INTERGOVERNMENTAL PARTNERSHIPS

When the current system of environmental management was created some 25 years ago, most state governments did not have the capacity to operate environmental regulatory programs. This is no longer the case. As the environmental regulatory system has matured, many states have developed strong programs. Two related reforms are now in order to help shift the focus from the narrow goal of environmental protection to the broader goal of sustainable development. The first reform is to move from a federally focused governmental decision-making structure to a collaborative design that shares responsibility among levels of government. The second reform is to shift the focus from centralized environmental regulation organized around separate programs to protect air, water, and land to a comprehensive place-based approach. It should be designed to integrate economic, environmental, and social policies to meet the needs and aspirations of localities while protecting national interests.

> *The new system will need to rely heavily on partnerships among federal, regional, state, local, and tribal levels of government.*

To accomplish these reforms, the new system will need to rely heavily on partnerships among federal, regional, state, local, and tribal levels of government. These partnerships will require unprecedented cooperation and communication within and among levels of government in a geographic area. For example, carrying out a community-designed sustainable development strategy may depend on close collaboration by a local economic development agency, a regional transportation authority, a state housing department, and a federal environmental agency.

This shift in focus to place-based partnerships will require major changes in the roles and responsibilities of federal and state regulatory agencies in communities interested in accepting new local responsibilities. The agencies should help build local decision-making capacity so that communities can begin to develop integrated economic, environmental, and social equity strategies themselves. Rather than simply issuing regulations from afar, these agencies will need to work in communities and provide information and technical assistance.

Along with the devolution of responsibilities to states and localities, however, some traditional responsibilities must be preserved. For example, the federal government must continue to establish consistent national standards to ensure uniform levels of protection across state lines. Greater flexibility is needed — not in the standards themselves, but to encourage greater efficiency in determining the means to attain such standards. In addition, in the development and implementation of place-based strategies, federal agencies must continue to represent and protect national interests that may not be represented by local interests in all cases. Examples include controlling transboundary pollution and protecting biodiversity.

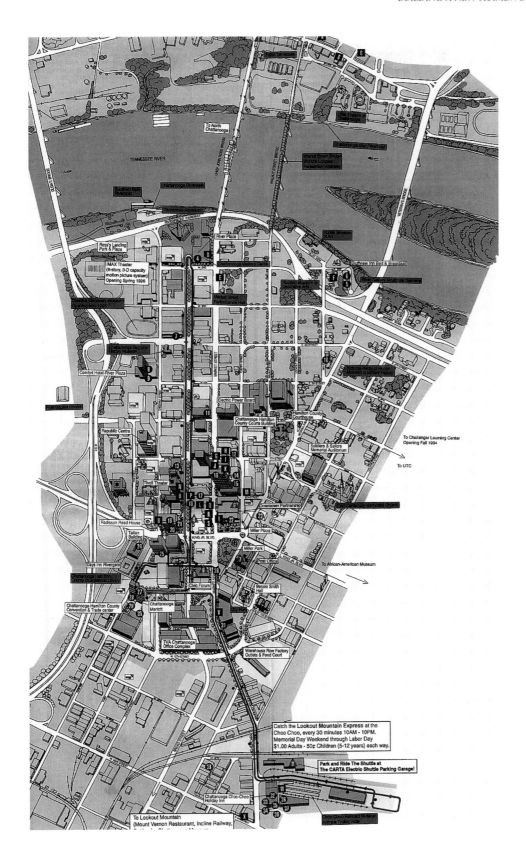

CHAPTER 3

INFORMATION AND EDUCATION

Information and education, in both formal and nonformal spheres, have a tremendous potential for increasing citizen awareness and ability to engage in decisions affecting their lives. Key to this strategy is managing information better, expanding access to the decision process, measuring progress toward societal goals more comprehensively, and incorporating accounting measures that educate and enable decisionmakers and individuals to make decisions that are more economically, environmentally, and socially sustainable. Additionally, the country's formal education system must be reformed to better address sustainability, and nonformal education forums and mechanisms tapped to promote opportunities for learning about sustainability.

THE CHALLENGE OF a new century offers the opportunity to create an educational, outreach, and informational system geared to the demands of a changing world, starting with basic and advanced skills and moving to job training and civic engagement. Equipping citizens with skills and knowledge will enable them to participate productively as members of local, national, and global communities. Continuing educational opportunities throughout people's lives — both in formal and nonformal learning settings — will enable them to adapt to changing economic conditions and respond to the need for environmental protection. Building a knowledge of the interdependence among economic prosperity, environmental protection, and social equity will help citizens understand, communicate, and participate in the decisions that affect their lives.

Information to Improve the Quality of Life

Building a knowledge of the interdependence among economic prosperity, environmental protection, and social equity will help citizens understand, communicate, and participate in the decisions that affect their lives.

Quality of life in a free society is determined by the collective decisions of its individual citizens acting in the home, the workplace, and together as members of the community. To make decisions that will help achieve the nation's economic, environmental, and social goals and improve the quality of life, people in all sectors of society need a solid grounding in the core academic subjects and access to lifelong educational opportunities, as well as accurate information about sustainable development. With education and access to quality information, citizens, government, and businesses are likely to find more efficient and equitable solutions to problems, to reach decisions that use economic and natural resources more efficiently, and to participate effectively in decisions concerning their families and communities.

Widely available information will become increasingly important as the United States moves to a new framework that places greater responsibility on individuals and the private sector to work cooperatively in making decisions that promote a balance among economic, environmental, and social issues. Informed decisions will create a more market-based regulatory framework — one that is more effective and flexible and less intrusive than the present system. The informed involvement by all government levels, the private sector, and individuals is needed to take such actions as:

- Establishing baselines for setting pollution reduction targets;
- Identifying risks and priorities;
- Developing innovative solutions;
- Understanding the consequences of individual actions; and
- Measuring progress toward economic, environmental, and equity goals.

MANAGING INFORMATION FOR SUSTAINABLE DEVELOPMENT

Accurate information is vital to sound decisionmaking, and the federal government has an important continuing role in helping to ensure the quality and integrity of public information, whether generated by government or the private sector. Citizens — both as private individuals and as members of the business community — depend on the quality and timeliness of information to alert them to hazards and to make informed decisions that promote economic and social welfare. As sustainable development focuses attention on new environmental, social, or economic concerns, government must perform this critical management function more effectively to ensure the quality and timely availability of new kinds of information.

Government already has collected an abundance of information, but often it is not available to policymakers or the public in a form they can use. This is the case with natural resources information, a subject explored in chapter 5, "Natural Resources Stewardship." A critical management issue is thus to improve the availability and usefulness of government information. Also, duplicative data collection should be eliminated, and data coordination and management should be improved. This will reduce costs and ensure that valuable information is not lost or wasted.

The federal government is already participating in collaborative efforts with the public, the private sector, and nongovernmental organizations to improve information management. These efforts should be expanded to include priority setting for data collection and analysis, identification of the most useful formats for dissemination, and additional mechanisms to help ensure that communities can obtain the information needed to guide sustainable development at the local level. At the same time, the federal government should work with the private sector to inform the public about consumer choices through disclosure of appropriate information in such areas as health, safety, the environment, and the social impact of products and services.

BETTER INFORMATION MANAGEMENT

Improve the collection, organization, and dissemination of information to reduce duplication and streamline reporting requirements while giving decisionmakers information related to economic, environmental, and equity goals.

ACTION 1. The federal government — working with state and local governments, private businesses, and the public — should thoroughly review and revamp how it collects, organizes, and disseminates data on economic, environmental, and social conditions and on demographic and health trends. The outcome should be improved coordination among federal agencies to better meet the needs of information users.

ACTION 2. Federal agency information system plans and programs should be included in agency submissions under the Government Performance and Results Act (GPRA).[1] Rather than manage their information-gathering and -processing activities by such elements as cost and the number of personnel involved, agencies have been directed under GPRA to manage programs according to their outcomes or products. This approach should be used to ensure that money spent by the federal government on information leads to the production and dissemination of information that meets the needs of the public and policymakers.

ACTION 3. The federal government should lead an effort to reduce duplication of information by integrating the efforts of various authorities. The U.S. Environmental Protection Agency (EPA) has launched a major effort to consolidate its reporting requirements into a one-stop format, initially through a Key Identifiers Project that will eliminate the burden on individual business facilities to report the same information multiple times on separate forms.[2]

ACTION 4. All levels of government should coordinate their programs on comprehensive regional inventories and assessments of environmental, economic, and social indicators of progress.

STRENGTHENING SCIENTIFIC INFORMATION

The ability to achieve sustainable development depends on scientific knowledge of the Earth's natural systems and the ways in which human activities affect these systems.

Accurate information built on basic scientific research establishes the foundation of knowledge needed for sound decisionmaking by individuals, businesses, government, and society as a whole. It helps people understand and predict changes in the environment, manage and restore natural systems, prioritize the potential risks associated with environmental problems, and take advantage of opportunities from technological developments. The private sector uses science to develop new technologies, production processes, and goods and services. In addition, baseline scientific data are critical to developing community-based sustainable development strategies.

POLICY RECOMMENDATION 2

BETTER SCIENCE FOR IMPROVED DECISIONMAKING

Strengthen the base of scientific knowledge and increase its use by decisionmakers and the general public.

ACTION 1. Government, the private sector, the scientific community, and nonprofit organizations should support or conduct long-term, independent scientific research to help decisionmakers understand sustainability issues, including the relationship among human and natural systems, human health issues, and emerging global problems such as global climate change and the loss of biodiversity.

ACTION 2. The federal government should promote international cooperation on scientific research related to sustainability.

ACTION 3. Current scientific research should be disseminated broadly and in ways that help policymakers, individuals, businesses, and communities make decisions that promote sustainable development.

ACTION 4. Government and the private sector should support and encourage research to improve risk assessment and cost-benefit analysis and to enhance their use as two tools among many in policymaking.

EXPANDING ACCESS TO INFORMATION

Information can be a powerful tool in making institutions accountable, building trust, and empowering citizens to take greater responsibility for economic and environmental improvement. Sustainable development requires that communities have the ability to compile and link disparate sets of data to create the information bases needed for effective decisionmaking.

For example, in the late 1980's the federal government for the first time required firms to disclose publicly the total quantities of hundreds of chemicals they released into the environment. The disclosures of toxic releases under the Emergency Planning and Community Right-to-Know Act quickly led to voluntary reductions — more than 40 percent in the first five years — and contributed to dialogue between companies and communities.[3] Many companies now voluntarily report far more broadly on environmental performance and invite community representatives to observe, evaluate, and help improve company operations. Implementation of the Emergency Planning and Community Right-to-Know Act demonstrates that complex data can be made available to the public in a manner useful to society. By illustrating a company's commitment to stewardship, these voluntary disclosures of Toxic Releases Inventory data also build credibility and public support for a more flexible regulatory process. Trust in open processes and broad disclosure and dissemination of information are central to sustainable development.

> *Sustainable development requires that communities have the ability to compile and link disparate sets of data to create the information bases needed for effective decisionmaking.*

Information — coupled with public education — is central to harnessing the power of the marketplace to reinforce more sustainable practices. For example, accurate product information, such as consumer product labeling and financial disclosure requirements, helps people make informed decisions regarding their personal and financial well-being. Accurate ecosystem data allow communities and regional areas to plan and carry out sustainable development strategies.

More efficient use of energy and materials by households is essential to making the United States more sustainable. The energy and natural resources used in American households have a significant impact on sustainability. With accurate information, consumers are more likely to make choices that save economic and environmental resources. Households also affect product design and manufacturing decisions through their purchases in the marketplace. If individuals are aware of the benefits and buy products that are cleaner to produce, use, and dispose of, they will reward the manufacturers, distributors, and retailers of those products by purchasing them. As individuals develop more environmentally and economically responsible consumer practices, they often become more aware of and active in bringing about the changes that local and national institutions need to make so society can reward those who use resources efficiently.

Sustainable development must be inclusive, and the Council believes that the nation cannot be divided between information "haves" and "have-nots" without major social inequities. Some individuals and communities have little access to information and lack the skills and training to make use of it. The issues of affordability and access to the National Information Infrastructure must be squarely addressed as key components of sustainable development. Further, training and community capacity-building are key components for widespread assumption of responsibility for sustainable development. Schools, libraries, nongovernmental organizations, governments, and the private sector are all central players in providing the necessary training and in building and sustaining the capacity of all communities to use information to support wise decisionmaking.

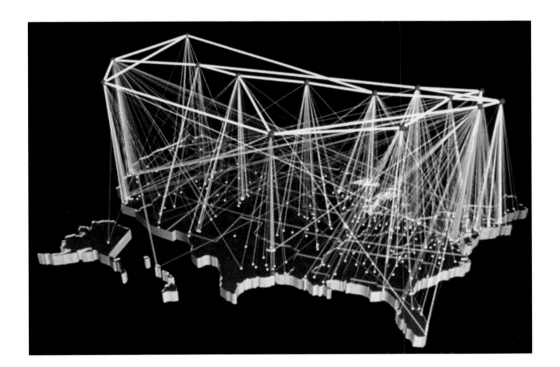

POLICY RECOMMENDATION 3

IMPROVED ACCESS TO INFORMATION

Adopt open information policies and practices, recognizing that disclosure and active dissemination of information should be the rule, not the exception. Adopt policies that increase access to public information for all segments of society and encourage the development of the National Information Infrastructure by the private sector in ways that improve access for all.

ACTION 1. New collaborative and flexible regulatory approaches require open processes to identify and communicate baseline measurements and improvements in environmental performance. All sectors must ensure that the new environmental management system recommended in chapter 2, "Building a New Framework for a New Century," provides sufficient access to information so progress can be tracked and verified.

ACTION 2. Individual, government, and business purchasers should ask suppliers to provide information on environmental characteristics of products and should factor these considerations into their purchasing decisions.

ACTION 3. The federal government should encourage agencies to ensure that the standards and formats used to provide access to public information are consistent throughout the government so that members of the public and policymakers can effectively search within and across agencies for information.

ACTION 4. The federal government, the private sector, and local communities should promote widespread public access to computers, computer skills training, and information available through computer networks such as the Internet to allow access to sustainable development information.

POLICY RECOMMENDATION 4

INFORMATION FOR SUSTAINABLE LIVING

Endorse and promote awareness of the economic, environmental, and social benefits of sustainable practices — such as more efficient resource use in government, the private sector, and the home — and encourage local governments, businesses, and community groups to engage people in making these improvements.

ACTION 1. The federal government should encourage and facilitate the creation of and access to information and data on sustainable development and sustainable living, such as ways to use resources more efficiently.

ACTION 2. Local governments, businesses, and community groups should create demonstration projects that increase citizen awareness of the effect sustainability has on the quality of life. These demonstration projects should help individuals identify opportunities to use resources more efficiently and achieve lasting measurable results.

BROADENING BUSINESS ACCOUNTING PRACTICES

Many businesses are integrating environmental concerns into all facets of their operations to increase their competitiveness in the global marketplace and to address public concerns about the environment. Environmental accounting can provide the information to help them identify opportunities to reduce both production costs and potential environmental threats through more effective environmental management.

Companies spend money to meet environmental objectives, whether on a voluntary or mandatory basis. Environmental costs include capital expenditures for pollution control equipment and salaries for staff who specialize in this area. Companies also spend money on the environment in other areas, such as operations and maintenance, labor, research, and marketing.

Unfortunately, standard business accounting practices bury the lion's share of environmental costs in non-environmental accounts and fail to trace costs back to the activities that generate them. As a result, managers often make crucial business decisions — what products to manufacture and what technologies and materials to use — without all the relevant facts. With a better understanding of a firm's actual environmental costs, managers and workers can identify opportunities to increase profits by using materials and energy more efficiently and so better protect public health and the environment.

Those who practice environmental accounting realize it is not a one-time exercise relegated to the periphery of a company. To ensure lasting benefits, it must be incorporated into ongoing business practices, including strategic planning, product development, and capital budgeting.

POLICY RECOMMENDATION 7

ENVIRONMENTAL ACCOUNTING

Develop and adopt accounting practices that link environmental costs with the products, processes, and activities that generate them to provide better information for business decisions.

ACTION 1. National business associations can work with their memberships to develop and adopt voluntary sustainable business practices, including accounting for the consequences of environmental practices and profitability.

ACTION 2. National business associations can provide technical assistance to small and medium-sized companies that are interested in identifying the range of costs associated with environmental management and innovative ways to reduce these costs while increasing environmental protection and economic productivity.

ACTION 3. Colleges and universities that offer degrees in accounting and business administration can offer courses on environmental accounting.

Education for Sustainability

Education for sustainability is the continual refinement of the knowledge and skills that lead to an informed citizenry that is committed to responsible individual and collaborative actions that will result in an ecologically sound, economically prosperous, and equitable society for present and future generations. The principles underlying education for sustainability include, but are not limited to, strong core academics, understanding the relationships between disciplines, systems thinking, lifelong learning, hands-on experiential learning, community-based learning, technology, partnerships, family involvement, and personal responsibility.

"Young people make up 20 percent of the population, but 100 percent of the future."

— Richard W. Riley, Secretary
U.S. Department of Education

Access to information is crucial in a democracy; but that information is useful only if citizens can put it into a framework of knowledge and use it to solve problems, form values, and make choices. That is where education comes in. Education for sustainability can give people the tools, skills, and experience they need to understand, process, and use information about sustainable development. It will help them make individual and collective decisions that both benefit themselves and promote the development of sustainable communities. And it will provide a means for creating a more highly skilled and globally competitive workforce and developing a more informed, active, and responsible citizenry. These objectives make it clear why education for sustainability is an integral part of the Council's long-term strategy for rebuilding communities and the country for the 21st century. How can education for sustainability be accomplished?

Education for sustainability must involve everyone. Education should flow from school to community and back again. Educators at all levels should reach beyond school walls, as many successful programs already do, to involve parents, industry, communities, and government in the education process. Colleges and universities should work with schools and communities — to deliver information, to identify questions for research, and to provide direct services to help solve community problems. For their part, communities should take a stronger interest in educating their citizens for sustainability, recognizing that current and future generations will need to be well-educated on this topic in order to bring about a sustainable future.

Education for sustainability must be a continuous process with widespread application. It thrives in all types of classrooms, exposing students to local, state, national, and international issues through hands-on, experiential learning in alternative educational environments — such as wading through streams to do water quality testing, volunteering in the community, or participating in school-to-work programs. Because sustainability is all-encompassing, learning about it cannot and should not be confined to formal settings such as schools, universities, colleges, and training institutions. Nonformal education settings, such as museums, zoos, extension programs, libraries, parks, and mass media, provide significant opportunities to complement and build on classroom learning. This means that formal and nonformal educators must work together to produce an educated citizenry.

Education for sustainability is about connections. Educating for sustainability does not follow academic theories according to a single discipline but rather emphasizes connections among all subject areas, as well as geographic and cultural relationships. Rather than weaken the rigor of individual disciplines, education for sustainability offers an opportunity to strengthen them by demonstrating vital interrelationships. For example, Dartmouth College requires students to take an international leadership course stressing business and environmental components. The Kellogg School at Northwestern University sponsors an elective course that involves a spring-break trip to places like Costa Rica to research such initiatives as the ecotourism industry and paper production from the waste products of banana processing. The Crouse School of Management at Syracuse University has a mandatory course focusing on what business students need to know about the environment; it also offers courses on land development law and environmental law as part of the business school curriculum. Students must strive to achieve high standards within the core disciplines, even as they develop an understanding of the connections across these disciplines. Further, education for sustainability involves a consideration of diverse perspectives, including those of ethnic groups, businesses, citizens, workers, government entities, and other countries.

Education for sustainability is practical. While delving into many disciplines, education for sustainability helps students apply what they learn to their daily lives. It engenders a sense of efficacy. Part of sustainability education is learning citizenship skills and understanding that citizens do have the power to shape their lives and their communities in light of their vision of a healthy and prosperous future.

Education for sustainability is lifelong. Continual efforts should be made to institute programs about sustainability in nonformal educational settings, including the workplace

and community centers and through the media. A citizenry knowledgeable about the benefits of sustainable living will have the capacity to create and maintain lasting change. Benefits to the individual include an understanding of and ability to participate in the social and economic changes that will affect their lives. For example, many communities have used planning processes that engage citizens in defining a desired future plan for their community. Using their plan, citizens work to achieve a sustainable future for themselves and their children.

An educated public is one of America's most powerful resources to meet the challenges created by increasing environmental, economic, and social demands. Our policy recommendations address both formal and nonformal educational settings and acknowledge the lifelong nature of effective education. These recommendations also address an array of crosscutting issues that relate to formal and nonformal education alike — such as technology, partnerships, equity, and international concerns. Together, these recommendations form a comprehensive educational strategy that promises to help lead the nation to a more sustainable future.

FRIENDS OF THE FUTURE

Seventh-, eighth-, and ninth-grade students from the St. Francis of Assisi School in Louisville, Kentucky, have created a voice for themselves and other youth in the state by forming Friends of the Future (FoF). With their teacher, Sheila Yule — who, according to one student, "pulls everything together and is the core of the group" — Friends of the Future members have set an ambitious local, state, and international agenda.

- *Locally, they are examining what they can do as individuals and as a group to protect and enhance the environment and their community. Students regularly conduct environmental testing and have alerted the city council to a variety of water quality problems in their community; in fact, they have helped prompt legislative changes to address the situation.*

- *Across the state, FoF members are working in partnership with a consortium of schools and universities, state agencies, and students from other environmental groups to develop strategies to better organize and incorporate environmental and sustainable development education into the Kentucky school curriculum.*

- *FoF's international mission is to raise awareness of the United Nations' Agenda 21 and of the role youth need to play in the discussion on sustainable development. Through the sponsorship and support of the U.N. Environment Program, FoF published the book,* We Got the Whole World in Our Hands: A Youth Interpretation of Agenda 21, *which documents the proceedings of the 1992 U.N. Conference on Environment and Development.[5] The book puts* Agenda 21 *into simple language — easy for younger readers to understand. The students presented their version at the national Earth Summit in Louisville in May 1993.*

REFORMING FORMAL EDUCATION

In the 1960s and 1970s, environmental education focused on natural resources conservation; in the 1980s, this curriculum was broadened to emphasize ecology and pollution control as well. Today, environmental education is evolving toward education for sustainability. Education for sustainability is not an add-on curriculum — that is, it is not a new core subject like math or science. Instead, it involves an understanding of how each subject relates to environmental, economic, and social issues. Educating for sustainability promotes both high standards of achievement in all academic disciplines as well as an understanding of how these disciplines relate to each other and to the concepts of environmental quality, economic prosperity, and social equity. But how should education for sustainability be transferred from conceptualization to practice?

Educating for sustainability does not follow academic theories according to a single discipline but rather emphasizes connections among all subject areas, as well as geographic and cultural relationships.

Educators — working in partnership with communities, businesses, and other stakeholders — can make education for sustainability a reality. Specifically, for various levels of formal education, they should define the skills and knowledge students will need in order to understand how various human actions affect the environment, economy, and equity. This understanding will be achieved most effectively if teachers make these connections to core academic subjects. Educators can encourage students to discuss these effects and form their own opinions. To this end, materials that incorporate hands-on learning methods — which can be highly effective in fostering an appreciation of complex, real-world issues — and that promote an understanding of how subjects relate to each other need to be developed. Finally, measures should be established to evaluate student progress in this area.

Because it is a relatively new concept for teachers as well as for students, education for sustainability needs to be incorporated into teacher preservice and in-service education programs. Wisconsin's preservice teacher certification programs, for example, include environmental education objectives; the state also has a large in-service program in environmental education. Both have elicited strong support from students, teachers, and school administrators. The Environmental Literacy Institute at Tufts University provides environmental literacy training to secondary school teachers and university faculty. The institute exposes participants to current educational theory, teaching strategies, assessment techniques, and information retrieval methods. Its nine-day participatory learning course covers such topics as life-cycle assessment, design for environment, cost-benefit analysis, market-driven technological innovations, and responsible industry practices. Today, teachers and professors in subjects ranging from English to engineering are incorporating environmental principles into their courses. Such programs offer examples of incorporating sustainability into educational training and teaching programs.

Colleges and universities also play a strategic role in educating for sustainability. Not only can these institutions develop curricula that integrate sustainability concepts, they can also incorporate these concepts into a wide range of activities, including research projects, career counseling, administrative procedures, procurement practices, academic curricula, and other university services. Through a partnership with the EPA, The George Washington University in Washington, D.C., is doing just that: sustainability concepts underlie much of its administrative and curriculum activities. The results of practical research or model greening projects conducted at universities and colleges also can be shared with the community and other school systems. *Blueprint for a Green Campus,* a collaborative effort of universities and colleges nationwide, describes ways to make sustainability a central focus of educational programs and to provide community and regional forums to discuss sustainability.[6]

POLICY RECOMMENDATION 8

FORMAL EDUCATION REFORM

Encourage changes in the formal education system to help all students (kindergarten through higher education), educators, and education administrators learn about the environment, the economy, and social equity as they relate to all academic disciplines and to their daily lives.

ACTION 1. Parents and representatives from states, schools, educational organizations, community groups, businesses, and other education stakeholders should identify the essential skills and knowledge that all students should have at specified benchmark grades for a basic understanding of the interrelationships among environmental, economic, and social equity issues. This could serve as a model for states and communities to use in setting their own requirements for academic performance.

ACTION 2. State officials, school administrators, and other educators and stakeholders should continue to support education reform; emphasize systems thinking and interdisciplinary approaches; and pursue experiential, hands-on learning at all levels, from elementary and secondary schools to universities, colleges, community colleges, and technical schools.

ACTION 3. Colleges and universities should incorporate education about sustainability into preservice training and in-service professional development for educators of all types, at all levels, and in all institutions.

ACTION 4. Schools, colleges, and universities should promote curriculum and community awareness about sustainable development and should follow sustainable practices in school and on campus.

GLOBE: HANDS-ON LEARNING

Students, parents, teachers, and school administrators met on the grounds of Jamestown Elementary School in Arlington, Virginia, awaiting the arrival of Vice President Al Gore, who was visiting the school to launch another GLOBE (Global Learning and Observation to Benefit the Environment) site. GLOBE, started by the Vice President in 1994 and supported by several federal agency partners — the National Science Foundation, the National Oceanic and Atmospheric Administration, the U.S. Environmental Protection Agency, the U.S. Department of Education, and

the National Aeronautics and Space Administration (NASA) — is designed to link teachers, students, and scientists around the world in a study of the environment. Says Jamestown principal Nicki Smith, "GLOBE is going to revolutionize education."

So how does GLOBE work? Basically, it is a hands-on scientific experiment. Teachers are trained to help students test soil, gauge air and water temperatures, study plant species and clouds, and measure the height and diameter of trees. These data are then posted on the Internet via the World Wide Web for use by students, scientists, and NASA. "It's exciting, electrifying," says Joseph Squeo, a fifth-grade teacher at Royle Elementary School in Darien, Connecticut, who is one of 12 teachers in that state being trained to run GLOBE programs at their own schools. "This program is unique because it makes students and teachers a part of a scientific experiment. We have ownership. We can get involved and be a part of the scientific study of the Earth. We're going to be doers and participants, and that is what is going to appeal to kids today."

To date, more than 2,500 schools in the United States and 32 partner countries have signed up as GLOBE sites. In order to be ready for the program's kick-off on Earth Day 1995, they planned and prepared for more than a year. Preparations included teacher and student training and creation of the necessary computer and telecommunications infrastructure in their schools.

Scientists are already benefiting from the information collected by the students. "We don't have the time or the capability or the research funding to do the work these students are doing," William Lawrence, a research scientist at the University of Maryland, remarks. Says Neal Pettingill, an 11-year-old Jamestown student involved with the program, "You're not just doing it to learn stuff, but you're actually helping scientists figure out what they need to help the Earth."

PROVIDING OPPORTUNITIES FOR LEARNING OUTSIDE THE CLASSROOM

People of all ages can learn about sustainable development in a variety of ways, including museums, zoos, libraries, extension programs, the media, their places of work, and community organizations. These nonformal educational settings can expand awareness and put concepts about sustainability in a familiar context. To be most effective in doing so, nonformal educational institutions need to work closely with formal educators to identify those areas in which schools are inadequately preparing students and to help fill those gaps and develop appropriate materials. This section highlights several nonformal settings that can play a key role in lifelong learning about and citizen involvement in sustainability.

It is crucial that the mass media be knowledgeable about sustainability and able to translate it into a language that everyone can easily understand.

Raising public awareness is central to any plan to move the nation toward sustainability. If citizens are to reverse such negative trends as urban sprawl, loss of biodiversity, and decreasing voter turnout, they must understand the issues and have accurate and accessible information about sustainability. In general, people rely on the mass media for their news and information. A 1995 Roper poll found that 72 percent of survey respondents obtained most of their news and information from television, 38 percent from newspapers, 18 percent from radio, and 8 percent from magazines.[7] Therefore, it is crucial that the mass media be knowledgeable about sustainability and able to translate it into a language that everyone can easily understand.

A national extension service, which collects and disseminates information on particular topics of interest, could be used to meet the research, technology transfer, and community needs generated by those interested in charting a sustainable course. It could make information on sustainability widely available to the public, schools, media, communities, and businesses and could clarify and infuse sustainability issues into the nation's environmental, economic, and social agendas. Various federal agencies have developed extension services that can serve as models for a Sustainable Development Extension Network: the U.S. Department of Agriculture's Cooperative Extension Service, the National Oceanic and Atmospheric Administration's Sea Grant program, and the National Aeronautics and Space Administration's Space Grant program. Alternatively, the existing Cooperative Extension Service could be restructured to focus on interrelated issues in communities, agriculture, forestry, manufacturing, and other economic sectors.

Community organizations offer another way to teach citizens about sustainability. Across the country, people are working in community groups to plan for sustainability. In Portland, Oregon, Chattanooga, Tennessee, and Seattle, Washington — just to name a few examples — citizens are participating in community "visioning" exercises. Through these, they typically envision a safe and healthy community with parks, walking and bike paths, good schools supported by parents and community organizations, affordable and clean housing, recreational facilities, museums, and libraries. They envision clean, energy-efficient transportation to replace traffic jams and road noise; and clean, safe, and friendly streets. These planning exercises are powerful tools in creating a sustainable future. By enabling communities to plan proactively — rather than function reactively — and by providing the information and technical expertise that communities need to realize their sustainable development plans, all citizens can help transform their neighborhoods into safe, healthy, and economically prosperous communities. Chapter 4, "Strengthening Communities," provides a detailed discussion about local initiatives, including community planning and goal setting, and training issues.

Educating youths and adults in the skills needed for the jobs and careers of the 21st century is a major ingredient in sustainable development. As jobs around the world become increasingly technology- and information-oriented, only those countries with an educated, skilled workforce will be able to achieve economic stability — the stability that in turn continues to provide jobs paying liveable wages. Thus, as the next century approaches, all citizens will need access to job training and retraining opportunities

COLOR ME GREEN

"People say, we're only children. People say, what can we do. Can't you see we are the future, and right now we're depending on you?" These are the words of songwriter Mike Nobel. They are powerful to read, but just imagine the impact when a group of students known as the Color Me Green singers put these words to music. Mike Nobel's songs and the Color Me Green singers are part of the Color Me Green campaign in Portland, Maine, to build awareness of environmental, community, and intergenerational issues.

Now in its third year, the award-winning campaign has been made possible by an enthusiastic partnership involving the local television station 6ALIVE, businesses, state regulatory agencies, environmental groups, educators, parents, and students. The campaign features four components: Nobel's songs, produced as music videos and aired as public service announcements; a series of "Ecotips," individual actions that people can carry out in the community; "Earth Notes" which describe current issues, such as what industries are doing to become more environmentally responsible; and a public education program that disseminates a Color Me Green school kit to schools throughout the state.

The Color Me Green campaign has been a huge success. The National Association of Broadcasters awarded it first place at the 1994 Service to Children Awards, and said that the campaign, "reflects the best of what America represents." And the fame of the Color Me Green singers is spreading. The group's recordings and videos have been circulated around the world and have received international acclaim. As one of their songs says, "'Cause everything we do today can change our tomorrow. And maybe when kids lead the way, the whole world will follow."

Color Me Green© lyrics copyrighted by Mike Nobel, Gorham, Maine, 1993.

throughout their work lives. This makes the workplace another important venue for nonformal learning about sustainability. For example, school-to-work opportunities offered through partnerships between industry and educators can help provide young people with the knowledge, skills, and career information they need for the future. Employers and educators should work together to determine and plan for current and future employees' education, training, and continuing education needs.

NONFORMAL EDUCATION AND OUTREACH

Encourage nonformal access to information on, and opportunities to learn and make informed decisions about, sustainability as it relates to citizens' personal, work, and community lives.

ACTION 1. Nonformal educators should encourage lifelong learning about sustainability through adult education programs, community and civic organizations, and nonformal education programs — such as those sponsored by museums, zoos, nature centers, and 4-H clubs — so that individuals can make well-informed decisions.

ACTION 2. Media strategists and sustainable development experts should develop an integrated approach for raising public awareness of and support for sustainability goals, conveying information on indicators of sustainable development, and encouraging people to adopt sustainable decision-making in their daily lives.

ACTION 3. A new or expanded national extension network should be developed to provide needed information to enhance the capacity of individuals and communities to exist sustainably.

ACTION 4. Local and state governments should continue to extend their partnerships with community organizations and other levels of government to support community sustainability planning processes and periodic assessments.

ACTION 5. Employers — in partnership with all levels of government, community organizations, businesses, educational institutions, and others — should develop training programs to create a workforce with the skills and abilities needed to adapt to changes brought on by the national and global transition to sustainability.

STRENGTHENING FORMAL AND NONFORMAL EDUCATION FOR SUSTAINABILITY

A variety of political, technological, academic, and social factors affect the success of any educational undertaking. Many of those factors affecting education for sustainability can be addressed through partnership, perspective, and access.

Local, state, and federal governments; parents, teachers, and schools; environmental organizations; and business associations should form partnerships to coordinate educational programs focusing on sustainable development. Such coordination should reduce duplication of efforts, increase availability of resources, and enhance stakeholders' knowledge and ability to make the decisions that will help their communities thrive.

Sustainability requires that learners of all ages be prepared for today's ever-changing, increasingly technological society. Computer-based instruction and hands-on experience can foster achievement in technological disciplines and increase employment opportunities. Consequently, in both formal and nonformal educational settings, equitable access to technology must be ensured.

Educating for sustainability requires that learners have an understanding and appreciation of the international forces that affect their lives. Environmental problems such as air pollution and pollution of the oceans are global in scale since ecosystems and ecological processes do not adhere to human-made boundaries. At the same time, economic and

social forces are becoming increasingly globalized. For these reasons, achieving sustainability will require cooperation on an international scale. If today's students are to be ready to make tomorrow's decisions, they must be able to understand the links not only among various subject areas but especially between local and global conditions.

Individuals from diverse backgrounds must have equal access to education for sustainability. Equally as important, their voices must be heard and their input included in the educational process. As the demographics of America's schools and communities change, it is essential that students learn to function in a multicultural society by understanding issues from various perspectives, resolving conflict creatively, and synthesizing new ideas from diverse points of view.

PARTNERSHIP FOR PROTECTION

"There are so many brilliant ideas, but they're like shooting stars because people do not figure out ways to make them sustainable," says Steve Hulbert, owner of an Olympia, Washington, car dealership and a member of the Council's Public Linkage, Dialogue, and Education Task Force. "A sustainable idea must have support and resources at all levels, otherwise the idea fizzles and fades."

So when Steve Hulbert had a good environmental protection idea, he knew its success would depend on strong partnerships with stakeholders from all walks of life. Olympia's watersheds affect many concerns; over the years, however, their viability has been increasingly threatened by human encroachment and activities. He joined with the Global Rivers Environmental Education Network (GREEN) and community members to develop a program that involves youth, businesses, educators, resource professionals, nonprofit organizations, neighborhoods, and government in monitoring the condition of the area's watersheds. The program's goal is to take watersheds from assessment to problem identification to rehabilitation to sustainability.

As part of this program, students from the North Mason School District are working with officials of the State Department of Natural Resources to assess the effects of heavily used recreational trails in the Hood Canal/Tahuya State Forest Watershed. Other partners in the program include the Puget Sound Water Quality Authority, the Washington State Department of Ecology, the Interagency Committee for Outdoor Recreation, the Washington state legislature, the Olympia Department of Natural Resources, and the U.S. Fish and Wildlife Service. These partners supply the resources and financial support while community organizations, businesses, and parents provide the volunteers. Together, they have also established an information network that allows resources, knowledge, and expertise to be shared.

Steve Hulbert's idea has turned into a full-scale program that uses national, state, and local resources not only to educate students about forest ecosystems, the connection between watersheds and the forest, and the effect that humans can have on both, but to empower the whole community to work together to take protective actions.

POLICY RECOMMENDATION 10

STRENGTHENED EDUCATION FOR SUSTAINABILITY

Institute policy changes at the federal, state, and local levels to encourage equitable education for sustainability; develop, use, and expand access to information technologies in all educational settings; and encourage understanding about how local issues fit into state, national, and international contexts.

ACTION 1. Federal, state, and local governments should form partnerships with private sector organizations, businesses, professional societies, educational institutions, and community groups to develop and implement coordinated strategies supporting education for sustainability.

ACTION 2. The public and private sectors should support the development of and equitable access to enhanced multimedia telecommunications technologies and improved clearinghouse capabilities that promote an understanding of sustainability.

ACTION 3. Educators in both formal and nonformal learning programs should help students understand the international factors that affect the nation's transition to a sustainable society.

ACTION 4. Formal and nonformal educators should ensure that education for sustainability invites and involves diverse viewpoints, and that everyone — regardless of background and origin — has opportunities to participate in all aspects of the learning process. This will ensure that education for sustainability is enriched by and relevant to all points of view.

CHAPTER 4

STRENGTHENING COMMUNITIES

Creating a better future depends, in part, on the knowledge and involvement of citizens and on a decision-making process that embraces and encourages differing perspectives of those affected by governmental policy. Steps toward a more sustainable future include developing community-driven strategic planning and collaborative regional planning; improving community and building design; decreasing sprawl; and creating strong, diversified local economies while increasing jobs and other economic opportunities.

FLOURISHING COMMUNITIES ARE the foundation of a healthy society. One measure of America's potential for long-term vitality will be the emergence of communities that are attractive, clean, safe, and rich in educational and employment opportunities. Sustainable development can easily remain remote and theoretical unless it is linked to people's day-to-day lives and seen as relevant to fundamental needs such as jobs, clean air and water, and education.

It is often easier to make these connections in the context of communities. It is in communities that people work, play, and feel most connected to society. Problems like congestion, pollution, and crime may seem abstract as national statistics, but they become personal and real at the local level: for example, people are frustrated by long commutes that take time away from family life. It is in communities that people profoundly feel the effects of shifts in the national and regional economy. Although decisions may be justified based on restructuring or other economic needs, workers experience the loss of wages to provide for themselves and their families when factories or military bases are closed. It is within communities that children gain basic education, skills, and training for jobs in the changing marketplace. It is within communities that people can most easily bring diverse interests together, identify and agree on goals for positive change, and organize for responsive action. While the challenges facing the nation are difficult to resolve at any level of government, local communities offer people the greatest opportunity to meet face to face to fashion a shared commitment to a sustainable future.

While the challenges facing the nation are difficult to resolve at any level of government, local communities offer people the greatest opportunity to meet face to face to fashion a shared commitment to a sustainable future.

The role of local communities is becoming increasingly important as the United States, and much of the rest of the world, moves toward more decentralized decisionmaking. The federal government will continue to bear the responsibility for bringing together diverse interests to establish national standards, goals, and priorities. The federal role is important and necessary in areas such as these because national interests may not always be represented in local decisions, and the effects of community choices are felt beyond one municipality. As discussed in chapter 2, "Building a New Framework for a New Century," the federal government is providing greater flexibility and expanding the roles played by states, counties, and local communities in implementing policies and programs to address national goals. This new model of intergovernmental partnership will require information sharing and an unprecedented degree of coordination among levels of government. Local government will play a key role in creating stronger communities — from planning and facilitating development, to creating community partnerships, to providing leadership.

and the ability to walk to obtain goods and services. This can result in decreased reliance on motorized vehicles, thereby reducing congestion and air pollution.

Sustainable community design is based on an understanding of the powerful effect of the built environment on aesthetics, scale, and a sense of history and culture. Historic buildings give society an important sense of tradition and education about the past. Preservation of existing structures also offers a way to reuse and recycle materials and related infrastructure. By rehabilitating older buildings, communities can save energy and materials and establish a sense of continuity.

Localities have used zoning and other ordinances to foster historical connections. For example, the bay windows contributing to the beauty and character of Boston's Back Bay were the result of a zoning code that allowed one-third of each building to extend to the street. Charleston, South Carolina, and Savannah, Georgia, among many other historic areas, have protected their architectural heritage — and enhanced their property values — by using design control measures and by making historic preservation a priority.

Some communities are working together to create regional strategies for transportation, land use, and economic growth. For example, in the Portland, Oregon, metropolitan area, communities are working together to plan for the explosive population growth the area has experienced since the 1980s. By using coordinated decisionmaking and establishing an urban growth boundary, which contains future growth, these communities are conserving open space and prime farmland to preserve the quality of life that has attracted so many people to Portland in the first place. They are also using community impact analyses to inform themselves about proposed development during the planning phase when adjustments can be made more easily.

Design that is coordinated among communities can help address issues related to growth. While some growth is necessary, it is the nature of that growth that makes the difference. Sprawl typically is development situated without regard to the overall design of a community or region. It often results in types of development — such as rambling, cookie-cutter subdivisions and strip malls — that perpetuate homogeneity, make inefficient use of land, and rely almost exclusively on automobiles for transportation. Sprawl development provides immediate and direct benefits to the people who move there, but the costs are longer term and borne by society at large. This is a "tragedy of the commons" in which individuals acting logically in their own interest harm a common resource. Sprawl is caused by a combination of incentives established by governmental policies and individual decisions made in response to a complex array of factors. This combination results in urban decline and is made worse by competition among local jurisdictions with little regional cooperation.

The brownfields issue is an example of the need for regional strategies. Brownfields are abandoned, contaminated, and/or underused land that is often found in the inner city. In contrast, greenfields are relatively pristine, undeveloped land, usually found at the edge of a metropolitan area or in a rural area. A company deciding whether to invest in building or modernizing a plant in a city center or building on rural or suburban open space weighs many factors. What is the cost of development? How much time will it take? What are the uncertainties? What are the operational costs? What is the proximity to the market or the workforce? Answers to these questions depend on a number of factors, such as labor skills and public safety concerns. The economic opportunities presented by brownfield redevelopment are discussed later in this chapter; but the issue of brownfields is clearly linked to sprawl, land use, and regional design as well.

Land use and infrastructure policies have a significant impact on development decisions. If the cost of cleaning up brownfields is borne by the developer but the cost of roads and utilities needed to serve greenfield development is borne by government, the scales tip. If the uncertainty of time and liability associated with brownfield development is greater, the scales can tip further. And if the tax burden in a newer, more affluent suburb is less than in the urban center, the case for greenfield development could be substantial. While it is a private decision made by individuals and businesses, it is greatly influenced by governmental policies that are not always readily apparent.

Benefits of developing open space are experienced one house or one business at a time. These benefits are tangible and immediate. The costs are harder to measure. In contemplating open land for residential or industrial development, an awareness and appreciation of what might be lost and of the environmental costs should be taken into account. Visionary planner Frederick Law Olmsted described urban parks as the lungs of a city.[4] This concept also applies to rural regions. Forests, farmland, mountains, plains, deserts, and swamps give the nation vital breathing room. New development should be based upon the carrying capacity of a region, which is the environment's finite ability to support life and renew itself.

Given the importance of the physical design of communities and their infrastructure, it is essential that communities continue to work cooperatively to understand and evaluate the potential long-term consequences of decisions made and to adapt them for their long-term well-being. State and federal governments should work collaboratively with communities to devise ways to measure these consequences in order to help local governments make their decisions.

Design, by definition, involves planning and making deliberate decisions. This occurs at different scales in the context of a community. The following recommendations are organized along these scales of design. The first scale relates to the design of buildings and other structures within the community. The second relates to the physical layout of streets, transit, residences, stores, and workplaces in the community. The third ties the community to others in the region.

POLICY RECOMMENDATION 3

BUILDING DESIGN AND REHABILITATION

Design and rehabilitate buildings to use energy and natural resources efficiently, enhance public health and the environment, preserve historic and natural settings, and contribute to a sense of community identity.

ACTION 1. Federal, state, and local governments should work with builders, architects, developers, contractors, materials producers, manufacturers, community groups, and others to develop and enhance design tools that can be used to improve the efficiency and liveability of buildings. These include models for building codes; zoning ordinances; and permit approval processes for residential and commercial buildings, public infrastructure, and landscapes. Model building codes should consider energy efficiency; durability; use of nontoxic materials; indoor air quality; use of recycled and recyclable materials; use of native plants that can reduce the need for fertilizers, pesticides, and water for landscaping; and use of designs that promote human interaction.

ACTION 2. These groups should disseminate these design tools, making the information easily accessible to local decisionmakers in interested communities which can use the model codes as a starting point, adapting them to reflect local conditions and values.

ACTION 3. Groups in communities that have made historic preservation a priority can inventory and prioritize historic properties and identify financing to rehabilitate these buildings. Local governments can enact ordinances to preserve historic buildings and remove incentives that encourage demolishing them. They can create incentives for rehabilitating and adapting historic buildings for new uses, where appropriate.

NOURISHING COMMUNITIES: JORDAN COMMONS

When Hurricane Andrew blew through Homestead, Florida, on August 24, 1992, it left in its wake $2 billion in damages and an immeasurable emotional toll on the rural and agricultural community. About 100,000 homes were severely damaged or destroyed, including more than 1,600 units of public housing. Today, the tent villages are gone and many homes have been rebuilt. Yet for thousands of low-income families, life has not returned to normal. With a continued lack of affordable housing, they still feel the effects of the storm in the most fundamental way. Homestead Habitat for Humanity, a nonprofit ecumenical Christian organization whose mission is to encourage private homeownership for low-income families, hopes to alleviate some of the shortage through Jordan Commons, a pilot project in community building.[5]

Jordan Commons will provide 187 single-family homes built with government support, $15 million in private donations, and the sweat equity of individual volunteers and future homeowners working side by side. As in all Habitat projects, homeowners will reflect the ethnic and racial composition of their community. At Jordan Commons, approximately 40 percent of the owners will be African-American, 40 percent Latino, and 20 percent white. Moreover, in addition to providing quality housing, the Jordan Commons project aims to tackle a much larger challenge. It hopes to use new principles in design and community planning to build a thriving neighborhood.

Eliza Perry, Homestead city councilwoman and Habitat board chair, describes some of the neighborhood's planned features. "The streets are designed for people. The roads will be narrow and the tree-shaded sidewalks wide. All homes will have front porches. Three small parks will allow children to play near their homes. The town center will draw homeowners out onto their sidewalks. This focal point of the community will house a 10,000-square-foot recreation center. Additional community buildings will hold a day-care center, a food co-op, continuing education programs, and an after-school program, all aimed at supporting families and encouraging social interaction."

Jordan Commons also plans to design environmentally sound homes. Scientists from Florida International University and the Florida Solar Energy Center have developed a list of energy-efficient approaches for building homes. With these innovations, the new homes are expected to be 38 to 48 percent more energy efficient than most homes of comparable size. Water heating will be supplied primarily through solar systems, and water will be recaptured and, after treatment, returned to the groundwater system. Alternative transportation will be encouraged through bike paths and racks, as well as a shaded bus stop station along nearby U.S. Route 1.

Underlying the thoughtful planning and family-friendly design is one central goal: citizen participation. As Dorothy Adair, Homestead Habitat president, states, "Simply building a community hall or neighborhood park does not necessarily create or encourage community. It is the common identity, public concern, and ultimately the collective action of residents that truly sustains and nourishes an evolving community. The facilities and services of Jordan Commons have been designed to engender such elements, and this is the true message of the Jordan Commons model."

POLICY RECOMMENDATION 4

COMMUNITY DESIGN

Design new communities and improve existing ones to use land efficiently, promote mixed-use and mixed-income development, retain public open space, and provide diverse transportation options.

ACTION 1. Local jurisdictions should structure or revise local zoning regulations and permit approval processes to encourage development located along transit corridors, near a range of transit alternatives, and in rehabilitated brownfield sites, where appropriate. Where there is demand for it, zoning should allow mixed-used development siting including residences, businesses, recreational facilities, and households with a variety of incomes within close proximity.

ACTION 2. Federal and state governments and the private sector should offer the assistance of multidisciplinary design teams to local jurisdictions that want help with sustainable community design. These design teams should include leading experts in a broad range of fields, including architecture, transportation, land use, energy efficiency, development, and engineering. Design teams should work with state and local governments and community residents with related experience to design, develop, and make accessible to communities alternatives to sprawl development, models for regional cooperation, and sustainable building practices.

ACTION 3. The federal government should work with lenders to expand research on location-efficient mortgages. Such a mortgage would increase the borrowing power of potential home buyers in high-density locations with easy access to mass transportation. A borrower would qualify for a larger loan based on expected higher disposable income from a reduction in or absence of automobile payments, insurance, and maintenance.

ACTION 4. Federal and state governments — in consultation with local government, the private sector, and nongovernmental organizations — should support local planning that integrates economic development, land use, and social equity concerns and engages significant public participation through existing planning grants. These principles, which were integrated in the Intermodal Surface Transportation Efficiency Act, should be reaffirmed during the act's reauthorization and expanded as requirements for federal and state funding and tax incentives for economic development, housing, transportation, and environmental programs.[6]

ACTION 5. The federal government should change federal tax policy to provide the same tax treatment for employee benefits for alternatives to driving as for employee parking.

ACTION 6. The federal government should give communities credit toward attainment of national ambient air quality standards under the Clean Air Act when they use community design

POLICY RECOMMENDATION 4

. . . .

COMMUNITY DESIGN

(continued)

to lower traffic by adopting zoning codes, building codes, and other changes that encourage more efficient land use patterns to reduce pollution from motor vehicles and energy use.

ACTION 7. All levels of government should work with community groups and the private sector to ensure that no segment of society bears a disproportionate share of environmental risks in a community. Collaborative partnerships could periodically conduct evaluations to ensure that desirable transportation and infrastructure investments — such as those in roads, buildings, and water projects — do not disproportionately deliver greater benefits to wealthier, more politically active communities and disproportionately fewer benefits to poorer, less politically active communities or communities of color.

PATTONSBURG: A TOWN RENEWAL

In Pattonsburg, Missouri, a small community of 250 that was nearly destroyed by the Midwest floods of 1993, a federally supported design team is working with residents to move the town — literally — to higher ground.

The community seized this opportunity to incorporate concepts and technologies for sustainability at all levels of their relocation scheme, from the physical structure of the new town to economic strategies for redevelopment.

Pattonsburg adopted a Charter of Sustainability — a set of principles to guide the town's development — as well as building codes to ensure energy and resource efficiency while preserving the community's character. It also created a privately funded Sustainable Economic Development Council to spearhead the expansion of environmentally responsible industry in the town.

Plans for the new town include use of the latest environmentally sensitive technology and eco-efficient design to meet the community's social and physical needs. The street layout is designed to be pedestrian-oriented and to maximize southern exposure to each home, giving residents the best opportunity to use passive solar heating to lower energy needs. A system of artificial wetlands will use the natural contours of the land to capture and treat polluted urban runoff, thereby saving money on sewer construction. A methane recovery system will help nearby swine farms convert an odor and pollution problem into energy.

Pattonsburg is an example of collaboration among local, county, state, and federal governments. It is also a noteworthy public-private sector partnership. Most importantly, it is grounded in broad-based community involvement and support. It shows how a rural community can turn tragedy into an extraordinary opportunity to shape a sustainable future.

eeeeeeeeeeeeeeeeeeeeeeeeeee

POLICY RECOMMENDATION 5

COMMUNITY GROWTH MANAGEMENT

Manage the geographical growth of existing communities and siting of new ones to decrease sprawl, conserve open space, respect nature's carrying capacity, and provide protection from natural hazards.

ACTION 1. States and communities should evaluate the costs of infrastructure in greenfield or relatively undeveloped areas to examine subsidies and correct market incentives in the financing of capital costs of infrastructure, such as sewers and utilities, for development of land bordering metropolitan areas.

ACTION 2. All levels of government and nongovernmental organizations can conserve open space through acquisition of land and/or development rights. For example, public water departments can budget to acquire land necessary to protect public water supplies. Private land trusts can expand their acquisition of wetlands or other valuable open space.

ACTION 3. Local governments and counties can create community partnerships to develop regional open space networks and urban growth boundaries as part of a regional framework to discourage sprawl development that threatens a region's environmental carrying capacity.

ACTION 4. Local governments and counties can work together to use community impact analyses and other information on the environmental carrying capacity of a region as the foundation for land use planning and development decisions.

ACTION 5. All levels of government should identify and eliminate governmental incentives, such as subsidized floodplain insurance and subsidized utilities, that encourage development in areas vulnerable to natural hazards.

ACTION 6. The federal government should redirect federal policies that encourage low-density sprawl to foster investment in existing communities. It should encourage shifts in transportation spending toward transit, highway maintenance and repair, and expansion of transit options rather than new highway or beltway construction.

CALIFORNIA SPRAWL

Unchecked development accompanied growth and prosperity in California over the past three decades. Today, along with many states and communities across the country, California must deal with the consequences of that kind of past growth — chief among them, the problem of sprawl. "As we approach the 21st century, it is clear that sprawl has created enormous costs that California can no longer afford," says the 1995 report Beyond Sprawl: New Patterns of Growth to Fit the New California. *"Ironically, unchecked sprawl has shifted from an engine of California's growth to a force that now threatens to inhibit growth and degrade the quality of our life."*

Sprawl takes its toll on society as well as on the landscape. The report identifies a variety of consequences. There is a dramatic increase in automobiles and time spent in traffic jams. Irreplaceable prime agricultural land and forest land are lost. Taxes and other costs for individuals and businesses increase to provide new infrastructure. Sprawl frequently widens the distance between where people live and work. It also results in abandonment of investments in older communities, which continue to suffer long-term decline.

This appraisal comes from a joint study undertaken by the Bank of America, California's Resources Agency, the Greenbelt Alliance, and the Low Income Housing Fund. It makes a compelling argument for reorienting growth to create more compact, efficient communities. The net effect would be to improve the business climate, conserve agricultural land and natural areas, and revitalize cities. Beyond Sprawl *sheds light on problems faced by communities not only in California, but in the Rust Belt and the Sun Belt, in the Midwest, Southwest, and Northwest.*

"This is not a call for limiting growth, but a call for California to be smarter about how it grows — to invent ways we can create compact and efficient growth patterns that are responsive to the needs of people at all income levels, and also help maintain California's quality of life and economic competitiveness," says the report. Community action, public policy, private business practice, and individual effort will all be necessary to attain this objective. The report also recommends multi-stakeholder collaborative efforts to create a constituency to build sustainable communities.

POLICY RECOMMENDATION 8

. . . .

ENVIRONMENTAL ECONOMIC DEVELOPMENT

(continued)

high-skill industrial jobs and sizeable sales revenues from manufacture of recycled products, and conserve landfill space. The federal government should work with state and local governments to establish related guidelines and model programs and create incentives to promote secondary materials use and recycling-related manufacturing.

ACTION 4. The public, private, and nonprofit sectors should work together to identify innovative opportunities to target some of the economic benefits from more efficient use of resources and greater regulatory flexibility in terms of creating jobs, opportunity, and social equity in communities.

CREATING CLEAN JOBS

Clean Cities Recycling, Inc. (CCR), is a nonprofit community development corporation formed as a joint venture involving 2-Ladies Recycling, Inc., of Hobart, Indiana; the Gary Clean City Coalition, a community-based environmental organization; and Brothers Keeper of Gary, a shelter for homeless men. CCR's stated mission is "to benefit the public interest and lessen the burden on government by creating permanent employment by utilizing the economic opportunities available through the processing and marketing of residential recyclables."

The joint venture was formed in 1993 to compete for a two-year contract awarded by the Lake County Solid Waste Management District to set up and operate 25 drop-off recycling centers. The district and its board were established in 1991, when Indiana set a goal of reducing trash to land-fills by 35 percent by 1996 and 50 percent by the year 2001.

To date, the firm has set up 10 drop-off centers at grocery stores. The sites are open Monday through Saturday, 8 a.m. to 8 p.m., and are serviced daily. They collect clean, source-separated household recyclables: glass, aluminum, steel cans, newspaper, cardboard, and some plastics. Materials are sold to local markets and established scrap dealers in the Greater Chicago area. Fiber is purchased by a paper mill in Lake County, glass is bought by a company just over the county line in Illinois, and steel returns to the steel mills.

Clean Cities Recycling now employs six full-time and two part-time workers who are paid $6.50 to $10.00 an hour. It provides job training, work experience, and letters of recommendation to homeless shelter residents, who are paid a stipend for their work. The venture also helps provide continuing financial support for Brothers Keeper. Benefits from the business flow to the city of Gary and surrounding communities.

POLICY RECOMMENDATION 9

REDEVELOPMENT OF BROWNFIELD SITES

Revitalize brownfields — which are contaminated, abandoned, or underused land — by making them more attractive for redevelopment by providing regulatory flexibility, reducing process barriers, and assessing greenfield development to reflect necessary infrastructure costs.

ACTION 1. All levels of government should work in partnership with community residents, environmental organizations, community development corporations, industry, and businesses to redevelop or stabilize brownfield sites by eliminating barriers and creating incentives for environmental cleanup and by reorienting existing state and federal economic development funding and programs to include these sites.

ACTION 2. Federal and state agencies should encourage investment in brownfield redevelopment by using the polluter pays principle, assuring prospective purchasers and lenders that they will not be held liable for cleanup in cases in which they did not contribute to contamination.

ACTION 3. The federal government should work with states, counties, and communities to develop tools that compare, on a site-specific basis, the local economic and environmental costs of developing a greenfield versus redeveloping a brownfield site.

REVITALIZING BROWNFIELD SITES

To make Cleveland, Ohio, the comeback city envisioned by civic leaders, urban revitalization has to overcome the barriers posed by brownfields — the contaminated and/or abandoned industrial sites found in many central cities. Cleaning up brownfields entails investments and risks that make the uncontaminated greenfields in outlying areas much more attractive sites for industry and other businesses. But unless brownfields are successfully redeveloped, there is little hope for a renewed and vibrant metropolitan core.

In the Cleveland metropolitan region, a coalition of businesses, community development corporations, Cuyahoga County officials, neighborhood groups, and other citizens is working to develop brownfield sites in the city. The number of vacant parcels of land in Cleveland increased from 9.8 percent in 1977 to 12.5 percent in 1987, according to the Center for Urban Poverty and Social Change. Filling up some of these parcels and redeveloping others in the face of such problems as increased and uncertain costs, liability, cleanup standards, and regulatory burdens has presented Cleveland with a strategic challenge.

The Cuyahoga County Planning Commission convened a symposium in October 1992 to discuss brownfield redevelopment strategies as part of an effort to counteract sprawl in the metropolitan region. Following up on the symposium, a multistakeholder Brownfields Working Group analyzed the problem of brownfields and made recommendations to the planning commission in July 1993. Since then, a voluntary cleanup law has been enacted in Ohio, and Cleveland has received funding from the U.S. Environmental Protection Agency for two demonstration projects. The planning commission is using a $198,000 grant from the agency to streamline remediation and redevelopment of at least three brownfield sites. As part of the project, the commission is to identify financial and regulatory barriers and recommend ways to remedy them. The project is expected to help cities across the nation resolve their own brownfield problems.

CHAPTER 5

NATURAL RESOURCES STEWARDSHIP

Stewardship is an essential concept that helps to define appropriate human interaction with the natural world. An ethic of stewardship builds on collaborative approaches; ecosystem integrity; and incentives in such areas as agricultural resources management, sustainable forestry, fisheries, restoration, and biodiversity conservation.

AMERICA IS BLESSED with an abundance of natural resources which provide both the foundation for its powerful and vibrant economy and serve as the source of aesthetic inspiration and spiritual sustenance for many. Continued prosperity depends on the country's ability to protect this natural heritage and learn to use it in ways that do not diminish it.

Stewardship is at the core of this obligation. It calls upon everyone in society to assume responsibility for protecting the integrity of natural resources and their underlying ecosystems and, in so doing, safeguarding the interests of future generations. Without personal and collective commitment, without an ethic based on the acceptance of responsibility, efforts to sustain natural resources protection and environmental quality cannot succeed. With them, the bountiful yet fragile foundation of natural resources can be protected and replenished to sustain the needs of today and tomorrow.

Without personal and collective commitment, without an ethic based on the acceptance of responsibility, efforts to sustain natural resources protection and environmental qualilty cannot succeed.

Stewardship will become more challenging, however, as the human population grows and its needs and expectations put greater pressure on the environment. As the population increases, so too will demands for fertile soil, clean and abundant water, healthy air, diverse wildlife, food, fuel, and fiber. And as the stresses on society intensify, so too will the need felt by individuals and families to turn to the natural landscape for beauty, solitude, and personal renewal. But if present trends continue and stewardship is not widely embraced, more people will face the results of having less available for them.

Recent years have presented Americans with examples of the apparent conflicts between human needs and the ability of natural resources to meet them. Some stem from use of or harm to resources once perceived as inexhaustible. Other conflicts stem from development decisions made when information was too sketchy to anticipate their full consequences. The depletion of once-abundant ocean fish stocks, the decline of Pacific salmon runs, the loss of old-growth forests, and struggles over the uses of freshwater supplies are clear reminders of the need today for greater stewardship of natural resources for the future.

Renewable resources — together with such nonrenewable resources as oil and gas, metals, industrial minerals, and building materials — contribute to the foundation of the economic and social development of the country. Conversion of these resources for human benefit has sometimes resulted in costly and unforeseen environmental consequences, many of which are only recently being fully recognized.

Public lands, including national forests and grasslands, national parks, national wildlife refuges, and rangelands, comprise a significant portion of the landscape. By statute, federal agencies are to administer these lands for the benefit of all Americans, including those who live near public lands or whose economic well-being depends on the goods and services these lands produce. Public lands are managed for multiple purposes; at times these purposes can conflict. Consider, for example, the many uses of public land resources. They offer extensive recreational opportunities, support millions of acres of cattle and sheep grazing, produce billions of board feet of timber, are the source of extensive energy and mineral resources, supply water to many metropolitan areas, and often represent the last remaining reserve for unique ecosystems and biological resources. Studies by the U.S. Department of the Interior's Bureau of Land Management have shown that the cumulative effects of past activities on public lands have led to serious environmental problems, including degraded aquatic and riparian systems; less productive rangeland conditions; fragmented plant, animal, and fish habitats; and decline in forest health.[1] Future stewardship of these public lands is critical to the economic and environmental well-being of many regions of the United States, and has important implications for the country as a whole as well.

Nonfederal lands comprise 71 percent of the acreage in the United States. Private landowners and state and local governments are responsible for the natural resources on nearly 1.6 billion acres of land. The majority of these nonfederal lands, almost 1.4 billion acres, are privately owned.[2] Thus, the commitment Americans have to conserving the natural heritage for future generations is best demonstrated through the stewardship of their own lands. Many owners of private lands have pursued ideals of stewardship, enhancing the economic and aesthetic values of the land, and giving both landowners and the community a sense of place. Private decisions on managing these lands have long determined the quality, vitality, and fate of natural resources and will continue to do so. Ecological integrity of the nation's natural systems will continue to depend on private choices.

Privately owned lands, however, are most often delineated by boundaries that differ from the geographic boundaries of the natural system of which they are a part. In some cases, therefore, individual or private decisions can have negative ramifications. For example, private decisions are often driven by strong economic incentives that result in severe ecological or aesthetic consequences to both the natural system and to communities outside landowner boundaries. The Council has recognized this barrier to achieving sustainable development. The key to overcoming it is to strengthen stewardship commitments through public policies and individual actions that reflect the principles of sustainable development and support for collaborative processes to enable landowners to enhance the value, productivity, and ecological integrity of their lands.

Although much remains to be done, the United States has made major strides in achieving a healthier environment and better protection of its natural resources. For example, by 1994, 14 million acres across the United States were protected through regional, state, and local land trusts. These private and voluntary efforts have produced a 49-percent increase in conservation acreage since 1990.[3] Citizens, environmental organizations, and government at all levels are working together to save precious natural resources while safeguarding jobs and local traditions. Actions to protect the bayous of southern Louisiana, Mono Lake in the Sierra Nevada Mountains, and striped bass in the Chesapeake Bay are but a few examples of collaborative approaches to natural resources stewardship. Soil conservation is another case in point. Faced with increasing soil losses due to erosion, Congress enacted the Conservation Reserve Program in 1985, which authorizes contracts with farmers to convert highly erodible cropland to less intense forms of production such as trees and permanent grasses.[4] Since then, 36.4 million acres, or 9 percent of cropland has been retired from crop production; on this land, soil erosion has dropped by 93 percent.[5]

Stewardship of the ocean's resources is also critical to the nation's public trust responsibility. Oceans provide jobs, recreation, and transportation to coastal communities, where more than three-fourths of the country's population are expected to reside by the year 2000.[6] The sustainable use of these marine ecosystems, as well as the species that inhabit them, is crucial to the future of these regions and the nation.

Ensuring that an environmental stewardship ethic is a guiding principle of natural resources management requires a lifelong commitment from individuals, communities, corporations, and the nation — today and for generations to come. How can society best develop and maintain a commitment to stewardship? The answer is multifaceted, but it starts with understanding the dynamics at work in the environment and the connection among environmental protection, economic prosperity, and social equity and well-being. It depends on the processes by which individuals, institutions, and government at all levels can work together toward protecting and restoring the country's inherited natural resource base. Education, information, and communication are all important for developing a stewardship ethic. Also important is the widespread understanding that people, bonded by a shared purpose, can work together to make sustainable development a reality. The following policy recommendations and actions offer ways in which stewardship can help move the nation toward sustainable development.

USING COLLABORATIVE APPROACHES TO MANAGE NATURAL RESOURCES

The collaborative decision-making processes described in chapter 4, "Strengthening Communities," can be particularly useful in the responsible stewardship of natural resources. Collaborative approaches can apply both to public and private resources when the decisions made on their use have broad implications for the whole community. What has become clear is that the conflicts over natural resources increasingly are exceeding the capacity of institutions, processes, and mechanisms to resolve them. Adversarial administrative, legal, and political processes are common venues for challenges to the many interests in natural resources. These processes typically stress points of conflict, dividing communities and neighbors. Litigation tends to be acrimonious and costly, often resulting in solutions that do not adequately address the interests of one or more key stakeholders. What is usually missing from the process is a mechanism to enable the many stakeholders to work together to identify common goals, values, and areas of interest through vigorous and open public discussion within the constraints of antitrust laws. The Council endorses the concept of collaborative approaches to resolving conflicts.

In its meetings and task force groups, the Council found that communities, citizens, and other stakeholders across the country are inventing and using their own collaborative processes. For example, stakeholders within the Feather River Watershed in northeastern California, an area containing portions of three national forests — Plumas, Lassen, and Tahoe — created a forum for people living there to use "common sense to achieve obvious goals: healthy forests and healthy small-town economies through time." Known as the Quincy Library Group (named for the library in Quincy, California, where it holds its meetings), the community-based group began by developing a management plan for the 2.5 million acres of prime federal timber land and is now working on steps to carry it out.

These types of groups are discovering and demonstrating that collaborative approaches, based on a framework of natural systems or defining land forms such as watersheds, offer useful tools for identifying common visions and goals for advancing stewardship and resolving conflicts. Experience is showing that they can serve as reliable means for addressing different interests; putting near-term problems in the context of long-term needs; integrating economic, environmental, and social considerations; building from but moving beyond the limits of narrow jurisdictions and authorities to adopt innovative solutions; and reflecting community interests as well as the interests of citizens elsewhere. Collaborative approaches envisioned here can give impetus to stakeholders and communities to make use of best available science in their decision-making processes, meet and exceed legal requirements for protecting the environment, monitor natural resources status and trends, and exercise collective responsibility for practicing and passing on a stewardship ethic.

Basing collaborative approaches on natural systems encourages people to identify with a particular place and take responsibility for it.

Basing collaborative approaches on natural systems encourages people to identify with a particular place and take responsibility for it. Frequently, people do not feel connected to a place or locale and so do not feel responsible for taking care of it. Decisions typically get made in fragmented ways, and the connection between individual lives and the health of an ecosystem can seem remote. Yet human activities are very much connected to the ecological integrity of a natural system, such as a watershed, and considering their effects within a framework based on a defining natural system can highlight cause-and-effect relationships; identify long-term implications; and lead to solutions that integrate economic, environmental, and equity goals. Construction practices that keep harmful sediments from accumulating in rivers and lakes help protect water quality for drinking and swimming, for example. Careful planning of a community's development along a lake or river can enhance property values, increase merchants' sales, add to people's appreciation of the natural environment, and protect wildlife habitat. The possibilities for recognizing and responding to these kinds of interrelationships abound.

Government plays a critical role in conserving, protecting, and restoring natural resources by setting and maintaining a foundation of strong environmental laws and regulations. Enforcement is an important component, particularly for pollution control. No single government agency or collection of unconnected agencies is sufficient. No set of statutes or regulations — however comprehensive and detailed — can take the place of the commitment by individuals and communities to protect natural resources and ecological integrity. Individuals, communities, and institutions need to work individually and collaboratively to ensure stewardship of natural systems.

Finding an acceptable integration of local, regional, and national interests is not without difficulty. Issues involving public lands and marine resources, for instance, require that a

POLICY RECOMMENDATION 6

RESTORATION OF FISHERIES

Restore habitat and eliminate overfishing to rebuild and sustain depleted wild stocks of fish in U.S. waters.

ACTION 1. The U.S. Department of Commerce — in conjunction with the National Marine Fisheries Service; the Regional Fisheries Management Councils; and other relevant federal agencies, state fisheries management agencies, and tribes — should develop fishery management plans that remove the human causes of fish population decline, including the elimination or mitigation of habitat degradation activities and incentives that encourage such activity. These plans should adopt the precautionary principle in decisionmaking that in the face of scientific uncertainty, err on the side of resource conservation.

These plans should address reduction in capitalization; improvement in the precision of science used for decisionmaking; quantitative assessments of social and economic effects associated with specific fisheries; public and private mitigating actions; reductions of bycatch, or sea life incidental to the catch of targeted species; improved cooperation and coordination among fisheries and land management agencies, private industry, hydropower agencies, and other stakeholders; and better programs to prevent accidental introduction of exotic species.

ACTION 2. The federal government, working with regional councils, states, and other stakeholders, should establish an allocation system for threatened U.S. fisheries as a possible fishing management tool. The system would set a limit on the number of fishermen eligible to work in threatened fisheries. In these cases, the stakeholders could explore a trading program that would enable fishermen to buy and sell the limited fishing rights. This action would create a cost-effective program for limiting fishing and thereby reduce pressure on endangered fish stocks. In determining whether to adopt a system of trading fishing rights, the economic impact on the industry must be considered.

THE RETURN OF THE ATLANTIC STRIPED BASS

In 1993, record numbers of striped bass, or rockfish, were hatched in the Chesapeake Bay, astounding scientists and creating a resurgence of one of the most important commercial and recreational fisheries on the East Coast. Striped bass migrate all along the Atlantic Coast, and most spawn in the tidal waters of the Chesapeake Bay, the nation's largest estuary.

Today's optimism stands in sharp contrast to the devastating conditions facing the Atlantic striped bass a decade ago. At that time, overharvesting and pollution led to a near collapse of the fishery and forced federal and state lawmakers to impose fishing restrictions. Notably, in 1984, Congress passed the Atlantic Striped Bass Conservation Act which allowed the Atlantic States Marine Fisheries Commission to develop a coastwide management plan to restore the striped bass. The plan called for severely restricted harvesting of the fish all along the Atlantic Coast, from Maine to North Carolina. Maryland took action within its fishing waters, imposing a five-year moratorium on harvesting striped bass beginning in 1985. Virginia followed suit in 1989. By 1990, promising signs of rebounding hatches allowed both states to lift their moratoria and the commission to ease its restrictions. Three years later, the number of young striped bass was the largest ever recorded. By 1994, the striped bass was declared a recovered resource, although special regulations are still in effect to ensure the fishery's long-term health.

The plan's success rested on the cooperation among commercial and recreational fishermen along the Atlantic seaboard, states and the federal government, and agencies within the federal government. The interagency, interstate cooperative approach taken is now considered a model for other fishery management plans. Says Bill Matuszeski, director of the U.S. Environmental Protection Agency's Chesapeake Bay Program Office, "It is a great example of how coordinated fisheries management, increased habitat, and improved water quality can bring an important fish species back from the precipice to an economically and ecologically restored state."

STRENGTHENING NATIONAL NATURAL RESOURCES INFORMATION

Information on the current condition of natural resources and related trends is vital to measuring national and site-specific progress toward sustainability. There are already numerous sources of natural resources data collected by many different government agencies, communities, tribes, private landowners, and others. Much of the information, however, is not readily accessible to public and private policymakers, managers, or interested citizens because it exists in different formats at different locations. The situation impairs the ability to monitor and assess long-term effects of management actions and to evaluate sustainability. This problem is particularly acute in the case of baseline data.

As discussed in chapter 3, "Information and Education," it is essential to make data more accessible, to make better use of the data now available, and to move toward compatibility of data from numerous sources. While actions to protect and restore ecosystems need to occur as more complete data are gathered, comprehensive inventory and assessment of the nation's renewable and nonrenewable natural resources and biodiversity are equally essential. These data can help provide a sound comprehensive basis for informing public and private natural resources decisions.

Many initiatives are aimed at improving compatibility and accessibility of natural resources data, including information that is comparable in terms of geographic and temporal scales in the computer-based analysis methods used. For example, interagency, regionwide ecosystem assessments are being conducted in the Pacific Northwest, the upper Columbia River Basin, the Sierra Nevada region of California, and the southern Appalachians. These efforts should be continued and expanded to include other regions.

Federal and state agencies and tribes can play an important leadership role by collaborating in the development of methods and protocols for data collection, analysis, display, and access. It is useful to build on past experience, such as the national natural resources surveys conducted for the past 20 years by USDA's Natural Resources Conservation

Service and Forest Service, and by the U.S. Fish and Wildlife Service. The national natural resources surveys and regionwide ecosystem assessments focus primarily on generic resource categories.[24]

In addition, there is the national network of Natural Heritage Programs which provides more detailed information on the distribution and abundance of plant and animal species and types of ecosystems. This network of state databases is the product of 20 years of partnership efforts involving state government agencies and The Nature Conservancy. The resulting Heritage Network offers a comprehensive source of data on biological diversity and is a useful complement to other resource databases.

The long-term goal for strengthening national natural resources information is to bring about better strategic and operational decisions at all levels of government and the private sector based on reliable, high-quality information that integrates economic, environmental, and equity considerations.

POLICY RECOMMENDATION 7

NATURAL RESOURCES INFORMATION

Strengthen information on natural resources by integrating and building on existing international, federal, state, and tribal natural resources and biodiversity inventories, assessments, and databases; and by developing and using compatible standards, methods, and protocols.

ACTION 1. Federal and state natural resources agencies should convene planning sessions among all stakeholders to agree on data and information uses, standards, and methodologies for collecting data and conducting assessments of the nation's biodiversity and natural resources stocks, and the formats for reporting such data and information.

ACTION 2. Federal and state natural resources agencies and private institutions can intensify efforts to collect inventory data, involving contractors, volunteers, and others in the process, and applying agreed-upon collection and reporting standards and methodologies.

ACTION 3. Federal and state natural resources agencies should establish accessible and useful data repositories.

ACTION 4. All those involved in collecting and reporting natural resources inventories can coordinate to develop indicators of sustainability and indices showing the status of efforts to achieve the sustainable use of resources.

ACTION 5. Natural resources managers can monitor their management practices on a voluntary basis. Independent third-party verification of biodiversity assessments and sustainable practices may also prove valuable.

ACTION 6. The federal government should support data collection and analysis efforts for migrating species that breed in the United States but winter in other countries.

CREATING PARTNERSHIPS FOR CONSERVATION

In areas that lie between densely populated urban land and protected wildlands, the interaction between people and their environment is critically linked to the protection of biological diversity and environmental quality for future generations. Owners of private property in these semi-natural areas are important participants in preserving biodiversity and creating sustainable economies. Future economic and ecological prosperity will depend to a significant degree on the ability to recognize and support the role that private landowners, in partnership with public and private conservation organizations, can play in promoting natural resources stewardship. Additionally, effective stewardship of biodiversity conservation can help prevent species declining to the point of endangerment and being listed under the Endangered Species Act.

Private voluntary partnerships can complement efforts under the existing system of laws that safeguard the environment and public and private protected lands, including conservation areas and preserves that provide an important measure of biodiversity protection across the country. The ability of future generations to make a living in these areas will be influenced by the extent to which private owners' efforts to conserve the landscape receive recognition and support.

Voluntary partnerships for conservation will benefit by drawing on three principles: sharing the lessons already learned about conservation on private lands, recognizing the successful efforts of those who have taken steps on their own property to demonstrate natural resources stewardship, and creating incentives that assist landowners in developing conservation strategies. Conservation easements, land exchanges, and transfer of development rights are types of mechanisms that can recognize the economic concerns of the landowner and the common goal of conservation. Use of these tools as a part of voluntary partnerships can help ensure that ecologically sensitive lands receive a measure of protection, complementing the nation's system of public and private protected areas, conservation areas, and preserves.

"THEY DIDN'T EXPECT APPLAUSE"

When Fred Annand and Al Hopkins made their presentation to a room filled with senior managers from The Nature Conservancy and Georgia-Pacific Corporation, they expected a long day of negotiations ahead. They were prepared for tense moments and heated debates. They anticipated high-energy discussions. What they did not expect was applause.

Fred Annand is a conservation manager in the North Carolina office of The Nature Conservancy. Al Hopkins is a senior forest resource manager for Georgia-Pacific. Their proposal called for the two organizations to manage 21,000 acres along North Carolina's lower Roanoke River, one of two remaining large forested wetlands on the southern Atlantic Coast. The area teems with deer, wild turkey, black bear, bald eagles, and bobcats and provides a resting ground for migratory song-birds, herons, egrets, and some 210 other bird species.

Annand compares the venture to navigating through uncharted waters. "This is a new arrangement for us. Georgia-Pacific will own the land, but all of the management activities, including timber harvesting on the seven tracts along the river, will be agreed upon by a joint ecosystem management committee." Hopkins reflects on the warm reception their idea received from both organizations. "We asked the group what they thought. They responded with a round of applause. That was a first for me, and I could tell by Fred's look that he was just as surprised."

On November 14, 1994, The Nature Conservancy Chairman John Sawhill and Georgia-Pacific Chairman Pete Correll, both members of the President's Council on Sustainable Development, agreed to implement the plan. Sawhill thought it made good sense: "We are very excited about this partnership. We believe in cooperative conservation. The Roanoke agreement is a prime example of how industry, private groups, and the government can work together." Bruce Babbitt, secretary of the U.S. Department of the Interior and a Council member, also praised the agreement, calling it "unprecedented, setting a new course for forest management. The importance of this agreement is that it proves that a forest products company and conservation interests can develop hands-on management partnerships."

Representatives from the U.S. Fish and Wildlife Service and scientists from North Carolina State University are members of the management team. Some tracts of the 21,000 acres will be deemed high priority because of their special ecosystems. On these lands, Georgia-Pacific has agreed to relinquish its timber harvesting rights. On other tracts, timber harvesting will take place, following methods agreed to by the joint management team.

Correll sees the partnership as an important part of the company's corporate mission. "I view sustainable development not only as a mandate for wise environmental and resource stewardship, but also as a responsibility to sustain a way of life. The Roanoke project is a good example of this. It's definitely a step in the right direction."[25]

POLICY RECOMMENDATION 8

BIODIVERSITY CONSERVATION

Create voluntary partnerships among private landowners at the local and regional levels to foster environmentally responsible management and protection of biological diversity, with government agencies providing incentives, support, and information.

ACTION 1. The federal government should provide incentive grants to landowners who act to protect and manage habitat for native species.

ACTION 2. Federal, state, and local tax laws, including estate and inheritance tax laws, should encourage private landowners to protect biodiversity by managing lands for conservation, improving degraded habitat, or donating land into protected status.

ACTION 3. State, regional, and local authorities can provide incentives to private landowners by targeting the use of bonds to finance the purchase, or protection through easements, of lands with significant natural value that are most threatened by incompatible uses. These funds should be used to capitalize trusts for protected areas, quasi-governmental conservancies, or other land funds wherever possible.

ACTION 4. State and local land trusts and conservancies can develop covenants among cooperating owners to maintain the long-term health and integrity of ecosystems. State and local land trusts and conservancies can enlist the cooperation of landowners in sustainable management patterns.

ACTION 5. Voluntary regional or watershed landowner councils can be formed to promote information sharing and cooperation.

ACTION 6. The federal government should recognize and encourage these efforts by creating partnerships with nonprofit organizations.

CHAPTER 6

U.S. POPULATION AND SUSTAINABILITY

Population growth, especially when coupled with current consumption patterns, affects sustainability. A sustainable United States is one where all Americans have access to family planning and reproductive health services, women enjoy increased opportunities for education and employment, and responsible immigration policies are fairly implemented and enforced.

THE PREVIOUS CHAPTERS of this report have addressed the various economic, environmental, and social implications of how people individually and collectively use resources in the United States. This overarching issue of consumption appears throughout the report — from our recommendations related to extended product responsibility and the use of market mechanisms to the development of sustainable communities, collaborative natural resources management systems, and an individual stewardship ethic. Understanding and addressing the unsustainable aspects of the nation's production and consumption patterns are essential to achieving the goals outlined in this report. But clearly, human impact on the environment is a function of both population and consumption patterns. It is possible for more people to have a smaller impact but only if — through changes in lifestyle or technological progress — each person uses fewer resources and produces less waste. Even if technological progress reduces the rate at which the United States uses resources and generates waste on a per capita basis, population growth will make the objective of sustainable development more difficult.

Production and consumption in the United States together form the critical link between population and sustainability.

With a population of more than 261 million, the United States is the third largest country in the world. As a result of natural increase, defined as the difference between births and deaths, and immigration, the U.S. population is growing by 3 million people each year, or 1 percent annually — more than twice the annual growth rate in most of Europe and in most industrialized countries, but far less than in developing countries. The U.S. Census Bureau projects that if current demographic trends persist, the U.S. population will reach 350 million people by the year 2030, and almost 400 million by the middle of the 21st century.[1] To put these numbers in perspective, under current trends, the United States is adding the equivalent of Connecticut's population every year and of California's every decade.

Production and consumption in the United States together form the critical link between population and sustainability. National quality of life derives in large part from the unprecedented scale of U.S. production and consumption. Production and consumption account for the throughput, or total mass of materials and energy that is used and makes its way through the economy, resulting in a U.S. gross domestic product (GDP) of more than $6.4 trillion in 1994.[2]

This high standard of living is also reflected in a high level of consumption — a level amplified by growth in population. The United States consumes more than 4.5 billion metric tons of materials annually to produce the goods and services that make up its unparalleled economic activity. (See figure 12.) One example of U.S. consumption patterns can be found in the energy sector. The United States has 5 percent of the world's population but accounts for approximately 25 percent of global energy use on an annual basis. There is greater opportunity for improvements in energy efficiency in the United States than in other industrialized nations; U.S. energy use per unit of GDP is

FIGURE 13

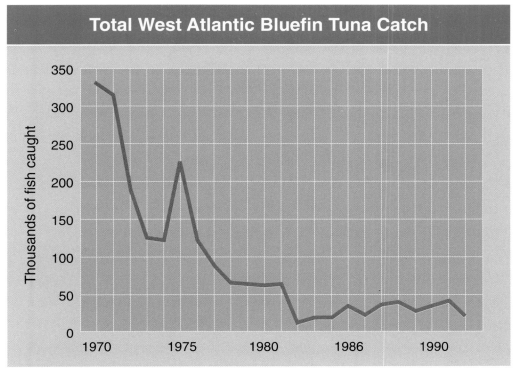

Total West Atlantic Bluefin Tuna Catch

SOURCE: International Commission for the Conservation of Atlantic Tuna, Standing Committee on Research and Statistics, *Draft Bluefin Tuna Working Group Report* (Madrid, 1993), table 2.

communities can only be solved, however, if nations agree upon common goals and shared responsibilities.

For example, the fishermen of many nations have competed for declining wild stocks of tuna, salmon, cod, and many other fish (see figure 13), a competition that recently flared into violent confrontation and international conflict.[2] The collapse of some fisheries brought misery to communities in the United States and elsewhere. No single nation can by itself limit catches to sustain the fisheries. All nations must agree to abide by the same rules to save the shared resource.

Forests — particularly tropical forests — play a critical role in maintaining the diversity, productivity, and resilience of global ecosystems.[3] Forests are also important national resources subject to sensitive issues of sovereignty. In response both to global markets for tropical hardwoods and domestic demand for land and materials, many countries are rapidly cutting their forests. Individual nations understandably resist calls to preserve their forests to provide global benefits. Only cooperative solutions based on global agreements will work.

Cooperation has worked effectively in structuring a phaseout of chlorofluorocarbons, the human-made gases destroying the ozone layer. U.S. industries responded to clear goals and economic incentives with a flurry of successful innovations that put them ahead of

FIGURE 14

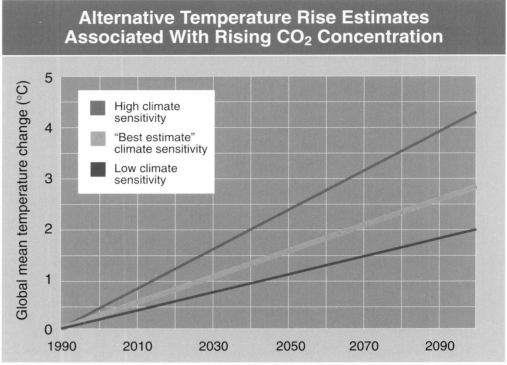

Alternative Temperature Rise Estimates Associated With Rising CO₂ Concentration

Legend:
- High climate sensitivity
- "Best estimate" climate sensitivity
- Low climate sensitivity

Y-axis: Global mean temperature change (°C)
X-axis: 1990, 2010, 2030, 2050, 2070, 2090

SOURCE: Intergovernmental Panel on Climate Change, *Summary for Policy Makers — Working Group I,* draft (Washington, D.C., 1995).

the agreed-upon schedule. The issues that demand international action include not only damage to ocean ecosystems and deforestation, but also — most importantly — changes in the atmospheric chemistry and composition that influence the global climate and loss of biological diversity. Each of these changes is proceeding at an accelerating rate with consequences that are difficult to predict with certainty or precision. Moreover, none of these phenomena can be quickly reversed after their consequences have been fully understood.

The Council heard a set of presentations concerning the science of climate change, the risks, and the uncertainties. Human activities are increasing the concentrations of so-called greenhouse gases. The models used by the Intergovernmental Panel on Climate Change predict a warming of 0.8° F to 3.5° F by the year 2100, although the resulting effects are much less clear.[4] (See figure 14.)

U.S. emissions of carbon dioxide, the primary greenhouse gas due to human activity, make up approximately 25 percent of global emissions of this gas; the per capita U.S. emissions rate is higher than that of any other major industrialized country and many times that of any developing country. In the future, emissions from the developing world will grow rapidly as their economies grow, and atmospheric concentrations of greenhouse gases consequently will rise. Without change, emissions from developing nations will surpass those from industrial nations — but not for several decades.[5] (See figure 15.)

FIGURE 15

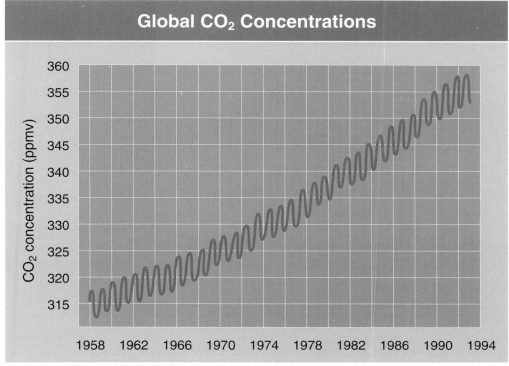

Global CO$_2$ Concentrations

SOURCE: Intergovernmental Panel on Climate Change, *Climate Change 1994 — Radiative Forcing of Climate Change,* J.T. Houghton et al., eds. (Cambridge: Cambridge University Press, 1995), p. 43.

It is clear that the United States cannot solve the potential problem of climate change alone. But it also is clear that unless the industrialized nations demonstrate the benefits of a different development path, there will be little incentive for the rest of the world to follow.

Threats to the global stock of biodiversity represent another global environmental challenge. Although the risks and implications for the United States (as well as its own contribution to the problem) may seem vague and uncertain, the economic and environmental effects could be profound. Economic benefits from wild species make up an estimated 4.5 percent of the U.S. gross domestic product. Fisheries contribute about 100 million tons of food worldwide. One-fourth of all prescriptions dispensed in the United States contain active ingredients extracted from plants, and more than 3,000 antibiotics are derived from microorganisms. Further, nature tourism generates an increasing percentage of tourism revenues worldwide. Yet, for all its value, biodiversity often takes a backseat in many economic development plans. Tropical forests house between 50 and 90 percent of all species on Earth, but because of forest clearing, 5 to 10 percent of the tropical forest species may be faced with extinction within the next 30 years.[6] (See figure 16.) Around the globe people who depend on the sea for a living are already witnessing a decline in the productivity of many of the world's most valuable fisheries. As with climate change, one nation cannot solve the problem alone, and the potential for economic harm is huge.

In accepting the challenges of leadership posed by its wealth, strength, know-how, and history, the United States must first adopt effective domestic policies to achieve sustainable development so that it can demonstrate that a better path to progress is possible. Falling short of its own goals may signal to the world the ineffectiveness of free institutions to create environmentally sound economic development that equitably distributes the benefits of growing prosperity. If the United States believes that free institutions are the best means for pursuing human aspirations, it must show that these institutions can respond to the great changes taking place.

More than 100 nations have established national councils on sustainable development similar to the U.S. President's Council on Sustainable Development; they seek to create consensus and shape policies to bring together economic, environmental, and equity goals.[7] Some, like the Canadian and Australian Roundtables, began their work several years before the U.S. Council. Most have been organized in response to the 1992 Earth Summit, the United Nations Conference on Environment and Development. Each of the councils is addressing the relationship of human well-being, economic progress, and the environment within the fabric of the conditions, needs, heritage, and politics of its own country. Their council representatives have said — in many different ways — that if the United States fails, they cannot succeed; but if the United States embraces the idea of sustainability, they believe their own nations will as well.

Because the United States is linked to the world by interrelated economic, environmental, and security interests, it cannot simply turn inward. The nation will achieve much that is in its interest by arguing the case for and assisting the transition to global sustainability. It can create markets for U.S. technology, foster equitable conditions under which U.S. industries and workers can compete, and build fair agreements for action to address global problems that affect the United States and its citizens. International engagement for sustainability is a task for government in its relations with other governments, but it is also a task for other parts of society.

For decades, and with considerable success, America has provided aid to nations to encourage development, fight disease, build democracy, and reduce environmental damage. The majority of that aid has come from government, but U.S. philanthropic organizations also have channeled billions of dollars of voluntary contributions into national and global efforts to meet human needs and protect the future. Leading U.S. companies have been influential in moving their industries toward openness and the application of consistent codes of responsible global stewardship. Nongovernmental organizations have helped to spur the creation of strong independent voices in debates on development, environment, and social policies around the world. Both official and unofficial roles are essential to the process of international change.

There must be several elements to this national engagement. One element is having strong and effective bilateral and multilateral development assistance agencies. Through organizations such as the U.S. Agency for International Development, the United Nations, the Global Environment Facility, and the various international organizations charged with helping implement the international environmental accords, the United

FIGURE 16

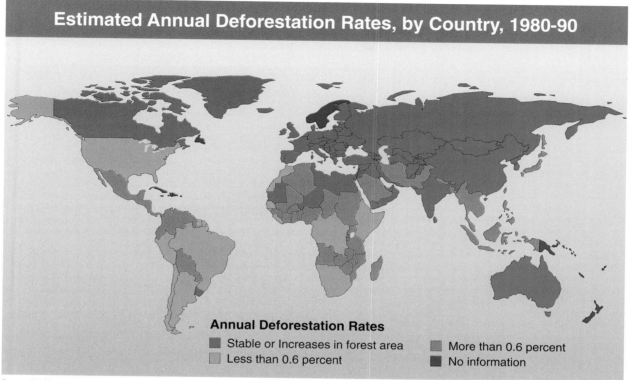

Estimated Annual Deforestation Rates, by Country, 1980-90

Annual Deforestation Rates

■ Stable or Increases in forest area
□ Less than 0.6 percent
▨ More than 0.6 percent
■ No information

SOURCE: World Resources Institute in collaboration with the U.N. Environment Program, the U.N. Development Program, and the World Bank, *World Resources 1996-97* (New York: Oxford University, forthcoming).

States can demonstrate its commitment to global development paths that make sense for both this country and the rest of the world. The United States can also continue to play a key role in helping developing countries confront the critical problems this nation has already solved at home, such as the removal of lead from gasoline and the development of environmental assessment techniques. Financial support is one way for the United States to make credible, substantive, and analytical contributions to the work of multilateral institutions and encourage broader participation by other countries.

Second, the United States is a signatory to the international conventions or treaties that are designed to promote common actions to reduce the risks of climate change and biodiversity loss — two of a growing list of international accords to address global environmental concerns.[8] Yet, the United States has not ratified the U.N. Convention on Biological Diversity — the only major industrialized country that has not done so — even though ratification was supported by a broad cross section of U.S. industry and environmental groups. As a result, the United States faces the risk of not being able to participate in the treaty or help shape the treaty's evolution. Further, the United States may forgo potential economic benefits from the import of genetic resources. The international environmental treaties may not be perfect from many different perspectives, but they do offer a framework for nations to use to move forward together when there is little incentive to move alone. America will derive the greatest benefit in support of its economic and environmental interests by participating in these treaties as well as in the full range of international development assistance processes.

Third, this nation must not diminish either the importance of scientific research for domestic and international fronts or the importance of the U.S. role in such research. To develop treaties to deal with new concerns and issues effectively, the scientific understanding of the problems and the possible responses to them must continue to be improved. Therefore, the United States should continue to support research and encourage other nations to participate more in international research on critical issues relevant to health and the environment.

Finally, but no less importantly, this nation should continue to promote and encourage global trading systems that mutually reinforce environmental protection and other social development goals. In recent years, initial steps have been taken to incorporate environmental provisions into regional and multilateral agreements designed to reduce trade barriers and improve equitable access to global markets. These agreements may serve to enhance U.S. economic well-being as well as that of other nations and to promote, in a broader sense, greater global stability. Much still needs to be done, however, in reconciling trade and environmental objectives in an increasingly integrated world economy. This is not just a job for governments, but requires the resources and commitment of the industrial community and the private sector as a whole. Improved economic health and political stability can provide greater resources for environmental protection and a more effective coordinated global approach to the challenges that the nations of the world face together.

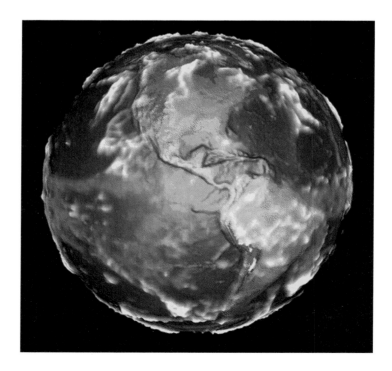

WILLIAM D. RUCKELSHAUS, Chairman, Browning-Ferris Industries, Inc. Mr. Ruckelshaus is chairman of Browning-Ferris, one of the nation's largest waste disposal companies, and until recently was the company's chief executive officer. He was appointed the first administrator of the U.S. Environmental Protection Agency in 1970, when the agency was formed. In 1983, he was reappointed to this post by President Reagan. He serves as a member of the Trilateral Commission and the Recycling Advisory Council. He also sits on the boards of directors of Cummins Engine Company, Monsanto Company, Nordstrom, Inc., and Weyerhaeuser Company. Mr. Ruckelshaus represented the United States on the United Nations World Commission on Environment and Development. He graduated from Princeton University and earned a law degree from Harvard University.

JOHN C. SAWHILL, President and Chief Executive Officer, The Nature Conservancy. Before joining The Nature Conservancy, Mr. Sawhill headed the energy practice of McKinsey and Company. He was president of the U.S. Synthetic Fuels Corporation and served as deputy secretary of the U.S. Energy Department in the Carter administration. Earlier, he was administrator of the Federal Energy Administration; associate director for natural resources, energy, science, and environment of the Office of Management and Budget; and president of New York University. He has served on the boards of several companies, including Consolidated Edison Company, Crane Corporation, and American International Group. Mr. Sawhill graduated from Princeton University and holds a doctorate in economics from New York University.

THEODORE STRONG, Executive Director, Columbia River Inter-Tribal Fish Commission. As the commission's executive director, Mr. Strong represents and is an advocate for the Warm Springs, Yakima, Umatilla, and Nez Perc tribes' ecosystem management philosophies and goals, which combine science and business acumen with traditional Indian values. Previously, Mr. Strong managed his own international trade and consulting company. Earlier, he was comptroller for the Yakima Indian Nation and president of the Native American Finance Officers Association. Mr. Strong is a member of the Yakima tribe.

EX OFFICIO MEMBERS

D. JAMES BAKER, Undersecretary for Oceans and Atmosphere of the National Oceanic and Atmospheric Administration, U.S. Department of Commerce. In addition to his duties at the Commerce Department, Mr. Baker is co-chair of the Committee on Environment and Natural Resources of the National Science and Technology Council. From 1993 to 1994, he was acting chair of the Council on Environmental Quality. Earlier, Mr. Baker served as president of Joint Oceanographic Institutions, Inc. He was co-founder and first dean of the College of Ocean and Fishery Sciences at the University of Washington and a faculty member at Harvard University. Mr. Baker was elected a fellow of the American Association for the Advancement of Science in 1988. He holds a bachelor's degree in physics from Stanford University and a doctorate in physics from Cornell University.

MADELEINE M. KUNIN, Deputy Secretary, U.S. Department of Education. Prior to assuming her present position, Ms. Kunin was governor of Vermont, an office she held from 1985 to 1991. After leaving office, she founded the Institute for Sustainable Communities. Ms. Kunin also served three terms in the Vermont General Assembly, and was elected lieutenant governor of Vermont in both 1978 and 1980. She graduated from the University of Massachusetts and holds a master's degree in journalism from Columbia University and in English literature from the University of Vermont.

RICHARD E. ROMINGER, Deputy Secretary, U.S. Department of Agriculture. Mr. Rominger's most recent occupation before joining the Department of Agriculture was as a family farmer near Winters, California. For his work, he was named Agriculturist of the Year at the 1992 California State Fair and received the California Farm Bureau Federation's Distinguished Service Award in 1991. From 1977 to 1982, Mr. Rominger headed the California Department of Food and Agriculture; concurrently, he served as president of the Western Association of State Departments of Agriculture and the Western U.S. Agricultural Trade Association. He also was a director of the National Association of State Departments of Agriculture and of the American Farmland Trust. He holds a bachelor's degree in plant science from the University of California, Davis.

TIMOTHY E. WIRTH, Undersecretary for Global Affairs, U.S. Department of State. As undersecretary, Mr. Wirth coordinates a broad group of global programs addressing, among other topics, population, environment, science, terrorism, and human rights. Previously, he was a U.S. senator from Colorado, assigned to the Armed Services, Budget, Banking, Housing and Urban Affairs, and Energy and Natural Resources Committees. He represented the 2nd Congressional District of Colorado for 12 years and was voted one of the 25 most effective members of the House. Mr. Wirth has served on the board of Denver Planned Parenthood, was a founding member of Denver Head Start, is a member of the Colorado Black Chamber of Commerce, and is on the advisory board for the Colorado Hispanic Agenda. He has bachelor's and master's degrees from Harvard University and a Ph.D. from Stanford University.

LIAISON TO THE PRESIDENT

KATHLEEN A. McGINTY, Chair, Council on Environmental Quality. Ms. McGinty is responsible for developing and advising on environmental, energy, and natural resources policy for the Clinton administration and for administering the National Environmental Policy Act. She was previously deputy assistant to the President and director of the White House Office on Environmental Policy. Before serving in the Clinton administration, Ms. McGinty was then-Senator Al Gore's senior legislative assistant for energy and environmental policy. In this position, she helped draft revisions to the Clean Air Act. She also served as congressional staff coordinator for the Senate delegation to the United Nations 1992 Conference on Environment and Development in Rio de Janeiro and as an official member of the U.S. delegation to negotiations on the Framework Convention on Climate Change and the Antarctica Protocol. Ms. McGinty has a bachelor's degree in chemistry from St. Joseph's University and a J.D. from Columbia School of Law.

PRESIDENT'S COUNCIL ON SUSTAINABLE DEVELOPMENT

The President's Council gratefully acknowledges the diligent service of the staff members and the principal liaisons, without whom the Council's success would not have been possible.

EXECUTIVE DIRECTOR
Molly Harriss Olson

STAFF
Carrie Beach, Correspondence and Scheduling Assistant
Shelley Cohen, Coordinator, Public Linkage Dialogue, and Education
Sally Cole, Former Chief Financial Officer
Linda Durkee, Writer
Peggy Duxbury, Coordinator, Principles and Goals
Joan Ebzery, Director, Legislative and Public Affairs
Julie Frieder, Coordinator, Eco-Efficiency
Susanne Giglio, Office Manager
Monica Gonzales, Coordinator, Population & Consumption
Liane Hores, Secretary/Receptionist
Kara Johnson, Former Secretary/Receptionist
Gary Larsen, Coordinator, Natural Resources
David Levine, Former Task Force Assistant, Eco-Efficiency
Eunice Lockhart-Moss, Special Assistant to the Executive Director
Jan McAlpine, Former Coordinator, Eco-Efficiency
Sarah McCourt, Director, Communications
Corinne McLaughlin, Former Coordinator, Sustainable Communities
Lois Morrison, Coordinator, Sustainable Agriculture
Angela Park, Coordinator, Sustainable Communities
Heather Sears, Former Correspondence and Scheduling Assistant
Sharon Segal, Chief Financial and Administrative Officer
Tom Super, Former Writer
Amy Todd, Former Task Force Assistant
Ed Wall, Former Coordinator Energy and Transportation
Greg Wedemeyer, Task Force Assistant
Kurt Zwally, Coordinator, Energy and Transportation

PRINCIPAL LIAISONS
Marcia Aronoff, Environmental Defense Fund
Frances Beinecke, Natural Resources Defense Council
Matthew Baca, State of New Mexico
John Bullard, U.S. Department of Commerce
David Gardiner, U.S. Environmental Protection Agency
Richard Goodstein, Browning-Ferris Industries, Inc.
Wade Greene, Rockefeller Financial Services
Lynn Greenwalt, National Wildlife Federation
David Harwood, U.S. Department of State
Jeffrey Hunker, U.S. Department of Commerce
Jane Hutterly, S.C. Johnson & Son, Inc.
Glynn Key, U.S. Department of the Interior
Keith Laughlin, Council on Environmental Quality
James Lyons, U.S. Department of Agriculture
Michael McCloskey, Sierra Club
Dennis Minano, General Motors Corporation
John Mincy, Ciba-Geigy Corporation
William Mulligan, Chevron Corporation
Rudy Oswald, AFL-CIO
Claude Poncelet, Pacific Gas and Electric Company
John Platt, Columbia River Inter-Tribal Fish Commission
Dirk Forester, U.S. Department of Energy
Russell VanHerik, The Nature Conservancy
Terence Thorn, Enron Corp.
Susan Vogt, Georgia-Pacific Corporation
Carole Wacey, U.S. Department of Education
Larry Wallace, Hazel & Thomas
Donna Wise, World Resources Institute
Ben Woodhouse, The Dow Chemical Company

ACKNOWLEDGEMENTS

The members of the President's Council on Sustainable Development would like to thank the hundreds of individuals and numerous organizations whose generous contributions of time, expertise, experience, resources, and funding made this report possible. Specifically, we would like to extend our appreciation to:

• The more than 400 additional task force members who greatly expanded the wealth of knowledge and perspectives upon which the Council drew in making its recommendations. Their efforts often involved significant contributions of time and energy, as well as financial and other resources.

• The thousands of people who attended Council and task force meetings and the hundreds who commented on the report at various stages of its development.

• The participants, volunteers, and contributors who made possible the Council's visits to Seattle, Chicago, Chattanooga, and San Francisco, enabling the members to learn from the unique experiences of these special communities.

• The talented group of experts and scientists who played an invaluable part in this effort by reviewing the numerous drafts of the report.

• The financial support of the many contributors who allowed the Council to carry its concept of shared responsibility for progress to the funding area as well. Corporations, nonprofit organizations, individuals, and government agencies contributed directly to the Council. In addition, scores of individuals and organizations contributed to nonprofit groups that enabled the work of the task forces.

• Facilitator, John Ehrmann of The Keystone Center.

• Editor, Nita Congress

• Fact-checking and Endnotes, James Stewart Schwartz and Alissa Schmeltz; Project Support, Elfranko Wessels.

PHOTOGRAPHY CREDITS: Cover Photography: © Paul Grabhorn; © University of Maryland. Page iii: NASA. *Introduction.* Page 1: © Bob Karey, NOAA/NESDIS. Page 3: © Paul Grabhorn. Page 9: EPA. *Chapter 1.* Page 11: © Paul Grabhorn. Page 13: © Paul Grabhorn. *Chapter 2.* Page 25: © Paul Grabhorn. Page 29: © Cliff Grabhorn. Page 31: © Paul Grabhorn. Page 37: DOE. Page 44: © Paul Grabhorn. Page 53: NASA. *Chapter 3.* Page 57: © University of Maryland. Page 59: NASA. Page 63: © Conna Cox and Robert Patterson. Page 65: USACE. Page 68: © Paul Grabhorn. Page 71: The GLOBE Program. Page 75: The GLOBE Program. Page 79: © Bill Weems, University of Maryland. Page 81: © Paul Grabhorn. *Chapter 4.* Page 83: © Paul Grabhorn. Page 84: © Melody Warford. Page 87: W.T. Sullivan from Satellite Photograph by U.S. Air Force. Page 100: National Park Service. Page 102: © University of Maryland. Page 106: © 1995 © Robert C. Boyer. *Chapter 5.* Page 109: © Paul Grabhorn. Page 111: © Paul Grabhorn. Page 113: PCSD. Page 118: NASA. Page 121: © Paul Grabhorn. Page 122: © Paul Grabhorn. Page 124: © Paul Grabhorn. Page 128: PCSD. Page 130: © Paul Grabhorn. Page 132: © Paul Grabhorn. Page 135: PCSD. Page 137: PCSD. Page 139: © Paul Grabhorn. *Chapter 6.* Page 141: © Paul Grabhorn. Page 143: © Paul Grabhorn. Page 149: Earthtrain. Page 152: © Hija Yu. *Chapter 7.* Page 155: W.T. Sullivan from Satellite Photograph by U.S. Air Force. Page 162: NASA. Page 167: © Paul Grabhorn. Designed by Grabhorn Studio, Inc.